f God and Man

Of God and Man

Zygmunt Bauman and
Stanisław Obirek

Translated by Katarzyna Bartoszynska

polity

First published in Polish as *O Bc...* 2014

This English edition © Polity Pre...

Polity Press
65 Bridge Street
Cambridge CB2 1UR, UK

Polity Press
350 Main Street
Malden, MA 02148, USA

ISBN-13: 978-0-7456-9568-6
ISBN-13: 978-0-7456-9569-3 (pb)

A catalogue record for this book is available from the British Library.

Library of Congress Cataloging-in-Publication Data

Bauman, Zygmunt, 1925-
 [O Bogu i człowieku. English]
 Of God and man / Zygmunt Bauman, Stanisław Obirek. – English edition.
  pages cm
 Includes bibliographical references.
 ISBN 978-0-7456-9568-6 (hardback) – ISBN 978-0-7456-9569-3 (pbk.)
1. Religion–History–21st century. 2. Spirituality. 3. Bauman, Zygmunt, 1925-
4. Obirek, Stanisław. 5. Dialogue–Religious aspects. I. Title.
 BL98.B3813 2015
 201'.5–dc23

                                                    2014049463

Typeset in 11 on 13 pt Sabon
by Toppan Best-set Premedia Limited
Printed and bound in Great Britain by CPI Group (UK) Ltd, Croydon

The publisher has used its best endeavours to ensure that the URLs for external websites referred to in this book are correct and active at the time of going to press. However, the publisher has no responsibility for the websites and can make no guarantee that a site will remain live or that the content is or will remain appropriate.

Every effort has been made to trace all copyright holders, but if any have been inadvertently overlooked the publisher will be pleased to include any necessary credits in any subsequent reprint or edition.

For further information on Polity, visit our website:
politybooks.com

Contents

Preface

This book is a dialogue about the dialogue: mostly about the underwater reefs that make its navigation anything but easy, smooth and tranquil in our times – times that render the mastery and practice of dialogue ever more imperative and urgent, perhaps more so than at any other time in human history.

This book arose out of an exchange of letters which started a few years ago, when awareness of the 'dialogical imperative', nowadays quite common and still rapidly expanding and deepening, was in its inception, struggling for recognition and admission to the public agenda inside which it now occupies such a prominent place and plays a pivotal role. That awareness has recently acquired an unprecedented momentum and commanded acute public attention under the personal influence of Pope Francis,[1] who – still as Jorgé Maria Bergoglio, an Argentinian bishop – warned about the dangers of breakdown of communication (between tribes, churches, political elites and hoi polloi), and presented unbiased, unprejudiced, open and cooperative (as distinct from combative) dialogue as the royal road to peaceful and mutually beneficial human co-existence. He noted in *Sobre el cielo y la terra*, a treatise published in 2010, that 'in order to have dialogue, you have to lower your defences, open the doors of your home and offer human warmth'; that 'the greatest leaders of God's tribe have been those men who have left room for doubt' and that 'true growth in human consciousness cannot be founded on anything other than the practice of dialogue and love'. And in his 'Annual Message to Educational Communities' of 9 April 2003, he wrote that 'The challenge of creative beings is to be suspicious of every discourse, thought, affirmation, or proposal that presents itself as "the only possible path". There are always others. There is always another possibility.'[2]

The dialogue reproduced in this book has a quarter-century-long history: its roots lie in the decision by Stanisław Obirek – more than thirty years younger than Zygmunt Bauman, and at that time a young priest and Jesuit though already a notable theologian, historian and cultural anthropologist as well as the editor of the Catholic monthly *Zycie Duchowe* (*Spiritual Life*)[3] – to invite Bauman to contribute to the series of 'Conversations with Non-believers' which Obirek initiated, conducted and published. In Obirek's own words, 'the difference between the worlds in which Obirek and Bauman lived struck them as so intriguing that they decided to juxtapose them and bring about a face-to-face confrontation [...] Looking back in an attempt at self-examination and of settling accounts with their respective life trajectories, both believed that there were alternatives to what is happening and did happen.' And as Zygmunt Bauman came to realize and tried to explain twenty years later at the start of their dialogue on God and man, 'we registered our spiritual troubles, our hopes of conquering them, and our visions of purification in different intellectual and institutional frameworks – but as to the logic of our paths, and probably also our experiences in our journeys through life – they are, I think, strikingly similar [...] Starting from different points, we nonetheless ended up in the same place.'

And so the book they offer their readers is an exercise in both theory and practice of dialogue: of the form of human togetherness probably as rich in its benefits as in risks and traps, but most certainly likely to deliver on its promise. It may not promise a life more comfortable, but it does promise a life more self-aware and self-controlled, as well as one benefiting from a better self-understanding.

1 Asked at the Vatican press conference of 16 March 2013 why he selected 'Francis' as his papal name, he explained that St Francis was 'a poor man who wanted a poor Church'.

2 All the above quotations are from *Pope Francis in His Own Words*, by Julie Schwietert Collazo and Lisa Rogak. William Collins: 2013.

3 In an interview given to Katarzyna Bielas of the Polish daily *Gazeta Wyborcza* and published on 17 December 2013, Obirek confessed: 'Joining the [Jesuit] order and taking holy orders, I was convinced of doing the best thing in my life. I felt the same way when leaving the order and resigning my ministry.'

I

Preliminary Measures

Stanisław Obirek   Our paths to agnosticism have been different. For years I persevered in the system, though I perceived its limitations. I had faith that it could be changed from within. Until I lost that faith. I now stand outside religion, but observe with great interest what is happening inside, particularly how it functions in the public sphere. Your biographical and intellectual adventures with religion emerge from a different background. Nonetheless, what you write, and how you write, about religion is extraordinarily fascinating. I would like Zygmunt Bauman to say more about religion, and in a more systematic way, maybe situating it more in your intellectual biography. Could we begin our conversation with a general sketch of this kind?

Zygmunt Bauman   Have our paths to agnosticism really been so different? Probably they have, in that the religions and churches whose limitations we perceived, but which we nonetheless believed 'could be changed from within', were different. But I suspect that the differences in our paths are limited to that ... We registered our spiritual troubles, our hopes of conquering them, and our visions of purification in different intellectual and institutional frameworks – but as to the logic of our paths, and probably also our experiences in our journeys through life – they are, I think, strikingly similar.

Moreover – and the moreover is important here – starting from different points, we nonetheless ended up in the same place. I have the sense that we understand each other from the first, and both of us consider the other's writings to be 'intriguing', maybe precisely because our spiritual paths have been marked by similar fears, similar conflicts, similar yearnings, often somewhat – or even fully – subconscious ones, and sometimes even completely unconscious...And these were paths from monologue to dialogue or polylogue, from the blind arrogance of the possessor of a single truth to the restraint of a witness to multiple human truths, from *monotheism* to...yes, exactly: *polytheism*. As I explain it to myself now, looking back: the 'limitations' you refer to stemmed from people from both churches entrenching themselves in fortresses of their own truths and slamming the door on any other truths and on anything that came into conflict with their beliefs, and on anyone who wasn't convinced of the infallibility and moral rightness of them – and then consenting to refuse the dissenters their right of resisting, and despising, banishing and ultimately annihilating those holding to different ideas or beliefs. Over those slammed doors an assertion was carved: if there is no God, everything is permitted. Though true to the fact, it should have said: if there is one God, then the people who are convinced of it are allowed to treat in any manner whatsoever those who lack or reject that conviction.

In brief, agnosticism (the kind that I, and I suspect also you, adhere to) is not the antithesis of religion or even of the Church. It is the antithesis of monotheism and a closed Church.

SO   Well, now we have the first question and the first answer behind us. That was the most difficult, at least for me – as the first sentence of Wisława Szymborska's charming Nobel acceptance speech was for her. After that, it may be easier. I will not conceal the fact that it gives me great joy that you perceive these significant convergences in our life circumstances. We will probably return to them more than once. I really like your way of framing our common, though very different, *monotheism*. I would speak less of *polytheism*, than of polyphony. Because after all, agnosticism, and in this case, restraint, demonstrates that we don't know whether we are dealing with one god or many. It is hard to say if they even exist at all. Leaving aside these unanswerable questions,

I would like to ask you to expand on the noteworthy aphorism that you concluded your last response with: 'If there is one God, then the people who are convinced of it are allowed to treat in any manner whatsoever those who lack or reject that conviction.' Is this actually how you see the relentless progress of monotheism (leaving aside the question of whether it is a religious or secular monotheism)? In that case, what would be the slogan for the evolving chronicle of the desire to discover the truth, the joys of discovering it, and the acute need to persuade others of it?

ZB Maciej Zięba OP uses the concept of a 'verital society' to describe this form of human co-existence, in which 'the entirety of individual life, from the cradle to the grave, as well as collective life' are organized 'around a universally acknowledged transcendental truth'.[1] And to make it clear what kind of form he has in mind, Zięba hastens to add that 'this does not only apply to Aztecs or the Maasai' (and, as he previously explained, also to Alkuin's project of *Christianitas*), 'but also to followers of Marx, Mao Zedong, or uncritical quasi-religious believers in physics or genetics'. And, I would add, the quasi-religious believers in the GDP, commerce or computer science. In each of these cases, God is *one*; this common feature marginalizes the differences dividing them and the various names and the images of origins or well-springs of the 'universally acknowledged transcendental truth[s]'. Every 'verital society' testifies to a war against diverse ways of life and their authorities; they all clamour for a monopoly on drawing the line between good and evil, virtue and vice, merit and guilt, orthodoxy and heresy, faith and paganism, truth and untruth. Zięba cites Karol Modzelewski's study *Barbarzyńska Europa* ('Barbaric Europe'): that which, in encounters with Christian missionaries, 'filled the barbarians with terror, was not merely a strange god, so much as the demands of monotheism. There is no lack of evidence that the pagans were willing to add Christ to their pantheon, they did not question his existence or his power...Mere baptism did not terrify. What terrified them was that the acceptance of the new faith was accompanied by the destruction of the old cult.'[2] On the other hand, according to chronicles and their interpretations by historians, Roman emperors with their politics of adding the gods of recently conquered places into the Roman pantheon, had no particular difficulties in assuring themselves of the obedience of newly conquered peoples. The only exception to that rule was, as we know, Judea – the one hatchery of unceasing rebellion and opposition – because it was also the only refuge of the idea of 'the one true God' on the territory of the Roman Empire; its people could not stand to have their God placed among others, who by virtue of their *otherness* alone could only be false pretenders to the divine throne.

Call it polyphony, if you prefer, or polytheism – a phenomenon that was well known long before polyphony was created; whatever you call it, the idea was associated with the peaceful co-existence of different modes of being human, whereas monotheism is coupled with the fratricidal struggle of these modes – a struggle to exhaustion or extermination. And in the idea of 'truth', regardless of whether it is attached to the word 'one' or lacking it, there is already a hard-to-remove suggestion of 'singularity', or at least its stipulation (I would even be inclined to say that the term 'one truth' is, like 'buttery butter', a pleonasm). 'Truth' is an idea that is, in its origins and its inalienable nature, agonistic – a concept that could only emerge from the encounter with its opposite: at a moment when a certain conviction ceased to be obvious (speaking more strictly, was pulled out from the haze of the unnoticeable by its clash with an alternative or a competitor). In Heidegger's words, once a previously inarticulate conviction (why would you articulate the unchallenged obviousness?) was pushed from the sphere of *zuhanden* ('given to hand') to the sphere of *vorhanden*: by virtue of being questioned, becoming a focus of attention, prompting thereby research and action. The concept of 'truth' wouldn't make any sense without polyphony or multiplicity of beliefs and perspectives, and so also a temptation to compete and a fight for dominance among contenders. The need for such a concept emerges at the moment when the claim 'It is how it is' has to be supplemented with the proviso that 'It isn't how others (whoever they may be) think it is.' 'Truth' feels at home in a *lexicon of monotheism* – and, in the final tally, of *monologue*.

From Holy Scripture we know that only God, precisely by virtue of his singularity, could introduce himself to Moses with the words, 'I am who I am.' All other contenders for a divine status were called, as common people are, by proper names; in other words, their *differentia specifica* assumed/signalled a

semantic family containing more than one member. The nameless-
ness of the God of Moses is the Bible's sole exception – and the
only conceivable exception. One wouldn't need a proper name
were one, as long as one remained, the sole being. The idea of
'truth' is a sort of Malleus Maleficarum – a hammer, yet, unlike
the 1487 Heinrich Kramer treatise, targeted not at witches, but at
unbelievers and doubters. It is only the missionaries and apologists
of the Biblical God who – once fallen into religiously pluralist
surroundings – were forced to argue for His *truth* (read: for the
untruth/falsity of all His contenders). Perhaps religious wars
stemmed from a search for truth; it is certain, however, that their
proclaimed objective was to provide proof for one's challenged
truth and to refute its challenges.

Maciej Kalarus, an exceptionally astute scholar of our polyphonic world and a tireless and fearless observer of its nooks and
crannies that are rarely visited by reporters or professional
researchers, demands that the word 'truth', similarly to words like
'scissors', 'goggles' or 'trousers', should only be used in the plural
(demanding by the same token also a *Lebenswelt* – the lived
world, the world of experience – of a kind that would allow for
such a usage). Indeed, using the word 'truth' in the singular in a
polyphonic world is like trying to clap with one hand... With one
hand you can give someone a rap on the head, but not clap. With
a single truth you can hit (and for hitting the adversaries it was
invented), but you cannot use it to launch an investigation into
the human condition (an investigation that in its very nature must
be conducted *only through dialogue*, or in the explicit or tacitly
presumed – but always axiomatic – assumption of alternatives).
Odo Marquard, a German philosopher of the neo-sceptical school,
half jokingly – but half in earnest – derives the German word for
doubt (*Zweifel*) from the number two (*Zwei* in German) and says
the following:

> When, in relation to the sacred text, two interpreters assert, in
> controversy, 'I am right; my understanding of the text is the truth,
> and in fact – and this is necessary for salvation – in this way and
> not otherwise', this may lead to a brawl and tussle [...] Could this
> text not be understood, after all, in still another way, and – if that
> is not sufficient – still another way, and again and again in other
> ways?[3]

A 'pluralizing hermeneutics', for which Marquard calls for a change, replaces a relationship dependent on 'the stubborn cling-ing to one's own truth' with an 'interpretive relationship'. This means, according to Marquard, with whom I am inclined to agree, replacing a 'being toward killing' (*das Sein zum Totschlagen*) with being toward the text...That step won't leave room for the invo-cation recalled by Zięba, and attributed variously to Arnaud Amaury or Simone de Montfort: 'Caedite eos! Novit enim Dominus qui sunt eius' (Kill them! For the Lord knows those who are his).

SO   Well then, let us talk about pluralism in religion. You men-tioned the 'pluralizing hermenutics' that Odo Marquard calls for when approaching sacred texts, or those considered sacred. This appeal is very close to my heart, and in the last few years I have been (pleasantly) surprised to notice it in the works of exegesis on these texts. In fact, arguably, even so-called 'monotheistic' reli-gions never really forgot their pluralistic foundations; rather, they were voiced in different ways. I think especially in Christianity, particularly in its Orthodox and Catholic variants. Because the Protestant Church, as it resisted what it saw as the blurring of the purity of monotheism, fought against cults of saints, sacred images and other such returns to a lost pluralism, or even polytheism. Is it not a fact that certain local saints have historically been more important than God or Jesus? And developed versions of the Marian cult have long managed to evade the strictures of mono-theistic purity. In particular, the 'legalization' of Marian sanctuar-ies and effigies is, to me, more an expression of resignation than of the development of the Christian religion. But let us return to the texts.

I will begin with the Hebrew Bible, because in some ways it does seem that, as you say, it is Judaism that bears the primary responsibility for ushering divinity towards singularity. But the situation is not quite so clear. Thus, for instance, Yochanan Muffs, the author of a remarkable book that is devoted to nothing more or less than the 'personhood' of God (*The Personhood of God: Biblical Theology, Human Faith and the Divine Image*) gestures to the complexity of the Divine Being. The author shows us that the God of the Hebrew Bible is not only *not* Aristotle's unmoved mover, but shines forth on every page of the Jewish Holy Book as a living Absolute, endowed with tenderness. In brief, the image of

God that emerges from Muffs' analysis, while shocking, is based not only on a precise analysis of Biblical text, but also on the religious context that it is embedded in. Muffs' position is not an isolated one, as I had previously thought. In it one can discern the voice of contemporary Judaism rooted in Talmudic interpretation. It is precisely through this kind of searching and laborious reading of the Hebrew Bible that the tragic face of God is illuminated. It is worth recalling the observation, gleaned from his studies, that Muffs shares with his readers: 'As Saul Liebermann [...] taught us, the truly tragic figure in the Bible is not Jacob or Saul or even Job, but God Himself, who is constantly torn between his love for Israel and his profound exasperation with them.'[4]

This is, in and of itself, a strange concept of God, both for religious people and for atheists. The former is puzzled to learn that the foundation of his faith could be seen in such a way, and for the latter the proposition is completely unfounded. If anything, the human condition can be described as dramatic, regardless of whether we are referring to a Transcendental Being or are content with temporal explanations. To me, the opinion of this brilliant scholar of Near Eastern religions is one of the most accurate claims about God that I have ever heard. It becomes comprehensible if we accept the idea that, in the Bible, it is not only man who is created in God's image, but also God – the creator of man – whose creation depends, for its success, upon the actions of man. As Muffs says:

> while the God of *agape* is human in His concern for mankind, He is not human in His independence. The law-giving God, on the other hand, is most human – too human – in His desire for the realization of the law, His frustration and anger over its nonfulfillment, and His willingness to allow mortals to control His anger so as to avoid destroying the world.[5]

This reminds me of the well-known Cabbalistic or Hassidic belief that the world's existence depends upon the existence of thirty-six righteous people. In this way, both God and humans determine the future of the world.

This motif of a mutual interdependence between Creator and Creations was always present in Jewish theological thought, visible in the earliest writings, such as the so-called 'Ethics of the Fathers'

(*Pirkei Avot*), which concern mankind first and foremost. So as to avoid making unfounded claims, I will refer to a few – actually the most famous – sentences attributed to Hillel the Elder, who may have been one of the spiritual teachers of Jesus of Nazareth. Hillel said, 'What is hateful to you, do not do unto your fellow', and added, 'be [...] a lover of peace, a pursuer of peace, one who loves the creatures and draws them close to Torah'. If these are the most important commandments of Judaism, where do the accusations that Jewish monotheism is the source of alienation, fundamentalism, hostility towards others come from? I am far from not seeing the symptoms of this religiosity in the Israel of today, but, after all, in them we can find not so much a measure of fidelity to tradition, as the degree of its falsification. I'm expressing myself in such strong terms because I am emboldened to it by a thinker whose ideas I hold close: Abraham J. Hesche, who based his entire theological system on the idea of 'God in search of Man'.[6] Regardless of how paradoxical the idea of God needing humans sounds, the basic premise of the Biblical covenant illustrates it. To again rely on Muffs: 'God's involvement manifests itself in His making a covenant with Israel. To some degree, man is copartner with God in establishing a moral world.'[7] One would like to add that this was not always obvious to God. It was only their mutual history that illuminated the true character of humanity to God – as a weak creature, but nonetheless necessary to the creation of the world. It is difficult, in such a framework, to discern the edifying character of religion or faith in God. It is rather a form of encounter and dialogue, in which the participants learn from each other, and above all respect their own limitations and differences. God does not feel morally superior to humans; rather, he is inclined towards greater leniency, which in the language of the Bible is generally called mercy. Or so says Muffs, in one final reference:

> Possibly God realized that if He is fallible in expecting the impossible from man and then punishing him, He better have more sympathy for human mistakes. [...] I am willing to suffer man's sinfulness, God says, to leave room for his humanity, for I cannot have my cake and eat it too: I cannot have a being free from sin who is also human. Rather a sinful human than no human at all.[8]

All well and good; one might think that this is a beautiful, but rather isolated (which is not to say false), interpretation of the Hebrew Bible. But another scholar of Biblical texts comes to Muffs' rescue: Israel Knohl, from the Hebrew University in Jerusalem, in his book about 'the Divine symphony', subtitled 'the Bible's many voices' (*The Divine Symphony: the Bible's Many Voices*). He is of the opinion that 'The editors of the Torah were the first composers of the divine symphony, which is embodied in the Bible and in Judaism as a whole. By transmitting to us the full scale and range of the different – and at times contradictory – choices, they have enabled us to listen to the divine revelation with all its fullness and richness.'[9] A particularly intriguing voice is heard at the moment that the name of God is revealed to Moses. I admit that Knohl's interpretation seems somewhat enigmatic, and is in any case at odds with a rather widely accepted view of the essence of the Jewish religion. We have been accustomed to associating it with a conviction of the uniqueness of the bond linking God and his chosen nation. Meanwhile, the

> revelation of the name 'YHWH' results in a theological Copernican revolution. Moses, and Israel with him, learns to recognize the essence of divine nature, which is unrelated to Creation or to humanity and its needs [...] Humans beings, when faced with the holy, no longer see themselves as the center of the universe, nor do they evaluate God from the narrow point of view of their own needs and desires.[10]

And, if this is the case, then who is God really, and why believe in such a God if there is no way to include Him in my life? This is the kind of question that could be asked by a person such as myself, who is outside of Judaism; but if I do actually believe, as I think I do, in the presence of God in the world, then maybe my religious agnosticism is not groundless? Maybe I am correct to view institutionalized forms of religion, which allude to Biblical revelation, with scepticism? Knohl, evoking one of the oldest traditions of Judaism, asserts that God gave humans their freedom, and carefully restrains Himself from intervening in human affairs: 'The School of Hillel represents a tendency – it may be called rationalistic – that seeks an autonomous existence for man on earth. "The Heavens belong to the Lord, but the earth He gave over to man" (ps. 115:16). The heavens cannot intervene in what happens on earth.'[11] I have to say that this very much appeals to me.

I fear, however, that in responding to you I've gone off in an unanticipated direction. But then again, we don't have to solve anything; rather, we are contemplating how to understand the world better. Maybe God, as He is understood by Biblical authors and Jewish commentators, doesn't interfere with that understanding. Or maybe he even helps? Am I mistaken?

ZB There are many layers to your presentation of the situation, Staszek, and each of them demands a different approach...I will start by saying that the idea of many gods is not the same as an inconsistency or multiplicity within one God. The Christian God is tripartite, and, from what I know of history, much blood has been spilled in affirming his one-ness in the face of that fact. I am not a scholar of the Scriptures, and am largely ignorant as regards the opinions of its commentators, but, from what I know (as an interested layman rather than an expert), exegetical scholars discovered at least three figures of God brought together in the Old Testament by its compilers: there is the Elohist God (who created the world and humans), the Jahwist God (who led the Israelites out of Egypt, in order to form a covenant with them and take them under His protection), and the Priestly God (the author of the laws to which He demands obedience in exchange for that protection). The compilers of the Torah did what they could to reconcile the irreconcilable, but they did not entirely succeed, and occasionally one glimpses the seams running through material intended to be unified/homogeneous. I think that they were aware of this, and that the ban on creating God's likenesses was a preventative measure or insurance policy against devotees of logic and its principles of non-contradiction and the excluded middle. Acknowledging the essential inconsistency of the one and only God is not quite the same as agreeing to multiple gods. The former issue may cause an internal conflict in a system of beliefs – though to a larger extent among its scholarly interpreters equipped with logic, to a lesser degree/extent in its guardians and overseers, and least of all among the *hoi polloi*, rank-and-file members of the congregation. The latter issue, however, is dictated by external forces: the presence of rivals, competitors or opponents endorsing *other* gods, who demand adherence to other laws and obedience to other interpreters and guardians. It is this second occurrence that makes the faithful aware of the need to speak out in the conflict between monotheism and polytheism. But it is this very one occurence, widespread and increasingly closer to home (every home!) in our globalized and diasporized world, that is crucial from the perspective of humanity. As a matter of fact, it is for this reason that I prefer to speak of 'polytheism' rather than 'polyphony' – an idea that already contains intentions of consistency and harmony being therefore fit for debating the first of these two problems, but not so much for seeking solution to the second. Such a solution, parenthetically speaking, does not have to develop as far as the concept of 'polyphony' would suggest – to a kind of organic harmony, or solidarity among discordant tunes (i.e., placing all the gods in one pantheon). It can rest content with achieving mutual tolerance: granting autonomy and renouncing the desire to impose one's own truths on others.

The other issue that you raise, the relationship between God and man, does not at all seem to me to be related to the issue of the monotheistic–polytheistic debate. In the idea of Creation as an act of God that is organic to the monotheistic system, man occupies a central position – if not as the purpose of Genesis, then as the instrument or crucial agent for its 'completion' or fulfilment. Human flurry, if I can put it that way, is a necessary ingredient/supplement to God's work; one could also describe this interdependence by saying that the hustle and bustle of humanity grants a retrospective meaning to God's Creation, though it may not have been one present in God's original plan (we will never know, because the God of the Gnostics – like *Ein Sof* of the Jewish Kabbalah, Infinite, Endless – was for many centuries before the birth of Kant's 'noumena' considered unknowable; I would say that it was precisely this acknowledgment of His unknowability that set God above mankind and drew a line between *sacrum* and *profanum*, the crossing of which was condemned as blasphemy or sacrilege). According to the Kabbalah, man can approach God's properties only through His *sefirot* and *parcufim* – emanations and faces, or, more specifically, manifestations and signs – and through that which man can manage to learn from them.

I am not, alas, a scholar of the Kabbalah, nor of Talmudic and rabbinic commentaries and (often highly contradictory) critiques.

Most of what I know of the Kabbalah comes from Gershom Scholem,[12] and I rely on his conceptualizations, while being aware that other interpreters (and recently they seem to be multiplying endlessly) promote other versions, trying to adapt their ideas to current New Age (or even neo-occult) trends. If one believes Scholem, in the Kabbalah (and even more clearly in Lurie's early modern summation of its Medieval strains), Gnostic explorations in the bosom of monotheism began with the paradoxes of which monotheism cannot rid itself: the singularity of God amidst the remarkable diversity of his creations, and God's goodness alongside the moral chaos of the created world. In some sense, the same paradoxes (or rather, the efforts to unpack them and overcome them) generated the myth of original sin, blaming the human exiles from paradise for the *tohu* ('chaos') befalling the world; unlike in the Kabbalah, which confronts humans with the task of *tikkun* – repairing a broken world and thereby restoring the harmony between God's creation and his purpose, and making this mission of humans into a part of God's plan. The world was broken through God's act of '*Tzimtzum*': initially identical with existence as such, God 'contracted' – retreated from a part of the universe – to make room for the human job of repairing it. What follows, is that, whereas the initiative to create the world was entirely God's, creation itself presumed from the very beginning that interdependence and cooperation between the Creator and his human creatures – which you describe, drawing on other sources. In opposition to Muffs, whom you discussed earlier, God did not err by overestimating human potential and their inclination to good; and it is not that the suffering that humankind experiences is meant to be God's punishment (revenge?!) for not meeting divine expectations. Quite the opposite, *Tzimtzum*, whose corollary was the creation of a space outside God's protection and goodness, was on the part of God an invitation to humans to cooperate in completing God's creation – an act of promoting humankind to the rank of co-creators of existence.

God's contraction, as Luria graphically deduces, shattered the earthenware vessels that contained *shekhinah* ('light'?, 'God's spirit'?), and the *Klippot* – shards or fragments of vessels – were scattered over the earth, placing people (particularly the people of Israel, giving sense to their being the chosen) in the position of having to collect and repair them: uniting the scattered and shattered sparks and glimmers of goodness into an all-encompassing flame. For the Jewish diaspora which the authors of the Kabbalah addressed and from which they themselves originated, *tikkun* implied recasting the exilic condition from being a punishment for sins into a redemptive calling: the redemption of men from the Fall, and protection of the world from falling.

Muffs chimes on this point with the Kabbalah: both assert that man is *God's co-partner in creating a moral world*, not an intended or unintended, successful or miserably crippled, product of that creation. In this partnership, I would say, God is the authority that shows the path and stimulates the journey; and man is who, having chosen God as an authority, is given a chance to progress in the indicated direction.

I found the most accurate account of this relationship in Levinas' reflections on 'the temptation of temptation' – as he described it, the temptation of *knowledge*: the state in which the tempted person may listen to the song of the sirens without giving up the return to Ithaca.[13]

The temptation of temptation is not an attraction to this or that concrete pleasure, to which the tempted risks surrendering body and soul. That which allures the tempted with the temptation of temptation is not pleasure, but the ambiguity of a situation in which pleasure remains a possibility, but the self still maintains its freedom of choice; it hasn't surrendered yet, it keeps its distance. There is the temptation of a situation in which the ego guards its independence, but that independence does not cancel the possibility of being consumed by temptation, elevated or debased. What allures is the simultaneity of externality and co-participation.

This kind of freedom, located betwixt and between the inside and the outside, portends the risk of evil, but also the possibility of conquering it. This is precisely, Levinas suggests, the 'temptation of temptation'; this is exactly what we crave, and for this we require freedom, or an indeterminacy extensive enough to contain the possibility of error and downfall. And this is exactly the possibility of the salvation of the world, through the resistance of evil, that mankind is tasked with. And this gift renders them co-partners of God in the creation of the moral world. Without man, this creation will not occur.

II

What about This Religion? On the Threat of Fundamentalism – Not Only the Religious Kind

Stanisław Obirek   Perhaps our opinions are beginning to diverge, particularly in reference to the question of the influence of the concept of religion, especially monotheism, on a person's life. This doesn't worry me at all, quite the opposite, because it allows us to clarify issues heretofore unnamed. Or so it seems to me. Zygmunt, earlier you said, 'The other issue that you raise, the relationship between God and man, does not at all seem to me to be related to the issue of the monotheistic–polytheistic debate.' But it seems to me that it is very important for us to realize that, despite the subtle assurances I've cited from Muffs and Knohl, the followers of a monotheistic God, whenever they have had the opportunity (and Christians and Muslims had it more than Jews, which is probably why it is less perceptible in Judaism), began converting others to their own truth in an entirely non-peaceful way, and this was connected to problems with their very understanding of monotheism. Despite an avowed faith in one God, in their day-to-day lives they did not become consistently monotheistic. I am no expert in the history of God, and I would not presume to paint with the broad strokes of Karen Armstrong in her *History of God*, a book that fills me with both awe and deep respect, but I would like to direct our attention to the so-called 'practical' side of monotheism, – namely, to life and the consequences emerging from it.[1]

I understand that the Jewish Cabbalistic tradition offers a remarkably subtle way of linking the divine with the human, and the Cabbalistic ideas that you discussed illustrate this beautifully. Nonetheless, as you well know, institutionalized Judaism viewed the speculations of Cabbalists with great suspicion, as indeed the Christian Church perceived the extravagant flights of its mystics, and as established Islam regarded Sufi practice. You refer to the studies of Gershom Scholem; perhaps it is also worthwhile to recall his student Moshe Idel, who both developed and enriched the findings of his teacher. You rightly point out the dilution of the fundamentals of Cabbalistic studies in today's popular culture, which not only trivializes, but even falsifies, the deepest dimensions of Judaism. Nonetheless, these caricatures should not be allowed to conceal the most important things in the Cabbala – that, in it, mankind not only meets God, but is even fused with him. If you'll allow me, I will mention a few ideas from Idel's book, which to me seems particularly inspiring in our consideration of what Russian thinkers have called God–human affairs. Idel approaches the Cabbala in a phenomenological way, but without bypassing the enormous hermeneutical tradition that has Paul Ricoeur at its forefront. I am thinking here of the one book of his that has been translated into Polish: *Kabbalah: New Perspectives*.[2] This is not only a work of astonishing erudition, but also one that asks weighty questions about the links between religious experience and its transmission in words, and about the place of that experience in different religious traditions, particularly those that emerged from the shared source of the Abrahamic faiths.

Idel examines some of these questions in many of his other books, which we do not need to discuss here, but I cannot resist mentioning *Messianic Mystics*, published in 1998, in which he pursues the topos of the messiah so key to Christianity, but considers it from a Jewish perspective.[3] This has significant consequences for Christianity's self-conception and perhaps this is why the book has not been unanimously well received among Christian theologians thus far. But let us return to new perspectives in research on the Cabbala. This is how he describes his intentions:

> My assumption is that the two main foci of Kabbalistic mysticism were the ecstatic–unitive and the theosophical–theurgical. While focusing primarily upon the descriptions of these two cores of

Kabbalah, I shall also take into consideration the historical development of these two themes recurring in Kabbalistic literature.
Thus my approach uses phenomenology in order to isolate significant phenomena only thereafter to elaborate upon the possible
historical relationships between them.[4]

It seems to me that this kind of distinction is fantastically important when describing the different, which is not to say divergent,
behaviours of Cabbalists. On the one hand, we see mystical strivings, whose purpose is somehow to 'touch' the Creator, and on
the other, an attempt to somehow wrest from Him specific behaviours towards the world. Both of these are amply documented and
there is no need to see them as opposed; rather, we should perceive
them as complementary. This is the way for us to learn how they
achieved *dwekut* – how they were able to reach the Creator
without losing their own lives.

In another chapter, Idel grapples with the rather deeply rooted
conviction that *unio mistico* contradicts Judaism, convincingly
demonstrating that it is precisely this mystical dimension of the
religion that brings it closer to both Christianity and Islam, and
maybe even to religions of the Far East. Interesting, too, is the
overview of different techniques of mysticism, which makes us
aware that we are not dealing with mere abstractions, but with
the concrete practices of adherents of different religious systems.
Particularly intriguing are the Cabbalistic theosophical analyses,
which illuminate deep ties between Christian thought and both
Gnosticism and Jewish creationism. Referring to the ideas of
Gedaliahu Stroumsa, Idel demonstrates how much of St Paul's
vision can also be found in Judaism itself. This pertains to such
fundamental ideas as the understanding of Christ as Image (Kol
1, 15–17), or as the Son of Man. Similarly fascinating are the
analyses of the concept of *du-parcufin*, which typically refers to
the bisexuality of humans, but in the context of Cabbalistic
thought refers to God and the phenomenon of *coincidentia oppos-
itorum* in God's very nature. Here again one can contemplate
whether Cabbalist thought could be a point of entry for a dialogue
between religions, whose subject could be the Jewish conception
of God and the Christian concept of the Holy Trinity. I apologize
for going on at length about the Cabbala, but my justification is

your incredibly intriguing interpretation of this aspect of Jewish monotheism. But enough about that!

I was recently struck by the sober observation of the French historian Paul Veyne, who made, in passing, what to me seems a very accurate claim. In his opinion, it is not the Abrahamic monotheisms discussed by Armstrong that deserve the name, but the religion of the Greeks. I admit that this greatly puzzled me, because I am accustomed to associating the Greek religious imagination with the highly populated Mount Olympus, not with the loneliness of a single God. I will allow him to speak for himself:

> [The Greek religion] is a monotheism worthy of the name, whereas the three monotheisms one currently speaks of are less worthy of praise. Ideas of their ancient provenance are misguided (the so-called monotheism of Jews was for a long time not the monotheism of a single god, but of one jealous of other gods, the gods of other peoples, gods existing according to him, and also according to his people, though of course Jahweh is stronger than other gods); misguided, too, are ideas of his true state of being (the Trinity, the Saints, and the Holy Virgin render Christian monotheism as a point of honor among theologians); also misguided are ideas of his reach (Allah is the only god, thanks to a myth that is just as accidental and arbitrary as the myths of polytheism, creating a desire to praise God as a monarch). Monotheism cannot be considered the central axis in the history of religion.[5]

The opinion of this historian allows me to offer a tentative criticism of your scepticism. It is precisely the impracticability of accepting monotheism and its translation into a plethora of tribal gods that leads the alleged followers of monotheism to fight so virulently against those who do not share their beliefs. Hence my conviction in the strong relationship between the worldly existence of humans and their religious passions. If people could agree upon the existence of a Single and Transcendent God, this 'mistaken' belief in tribal gods would merely be seen as one of many, similar to people's – after all, limited – postulations about the Unreachable and Inconceivable. But this way, by comparing their own ideas to those of others, they are ready to fight, and not just to first blood, but without stopping until they destroy their adversary.

This is what I accuse today's monotheisms of, that they have renounced the fundamental inspiration and intuitions of their forefathers and become practising polytheists. This is also why I look longingly back to the Greeks, who could afford an interest in and ability to draw from different sources, rather than remaining content with their own 'reserves of faith'.

I also want to say something about the Levinas text that you referred to. I am not sure that I understand the essence of the 'temptation of temptation' and the consequences for human freedom emerging from it, or the possibility of becoming God's co-partner in the creation of a moral world, or, using the language of theologians, its salvation. If I can offer my own vision of this salvation of the world, in my understanding it has a remarkably immanent character and takes place here on earth – not within me as Levinas would have it (or so I understand the fragment you referred to), but in the encounter with a concrete person. In my case, there are many of these people, and it is precisely friendship, love and the deep understanding that I receive and reciprocate, that leads to the world being a better place, and our lives becoming worth living. This way of 'redeeming the world' has nothing to do with my religious convictions, which are simply ways of experiencing the world that are inherited and passed on in families. But it in no way interferes with that; in fact, I often find it fascinating how the people closest to me get by without evoking these transcendental ideas. This in no way diminishes their participation in the 'redemption of the world', at least not in the way I understand it.

Does this mean that differences aren't meaningful and that everything becomes liquid or changes colours based on context and the experience of the here and now? That is certainly how I live my life. I don't know, maybe it's due to your influence, Zygmunt, and your concept of the liquid. I also must warn you that I do not see myself as a victim of the muddling of culture and worldview that happened, on your account as well, in the last decade. It often seems to me that, thanks to these descriptions of the world as liquid reality, we are closer to life...

Zygmunt Bauman I stand no chance of competing with your erudition in religion and religious literature, and for the umpteenth time can only bow my head in admiration. I will limit myself to remarking that what in my opinion sometimes diverts our exchange onto a sidetrack, and occasionally makes us speak past each other rather than to each other, is the misunderstanding lurking in the quote from Veyne you gave earlier: 'the so-called monotheism of Jews was for a long time not the monotheism of a single god, but of one jealous of other gods, the gods of other peoples, gods existing according to him, and also according to his people, though of course Jahweh is stronger than other gods'. I am not sure whether this is what Veyne intended, but the above formulation implies a contradiction between monotheism and the acknowledgment of the presence of other gods – be they usurpers or false pretenders. I believe that it is exactly the other way around: monotheism, much like truth, is an *agonistic idea* and can only function in the context of a battle-to-the-end. Much like the idea of truth (by definition 'singular'), born of multiplicity of opinions and the necessity of choosing among them, and redundant in a hypothetical case of absolute, universal consensus, the insistence on the singularity of God obliquely attests to the presence of other opinions and to the intention to outlaw them. Jews and Muslims constantly reiterate that Adonai or Allah is one and only because, much like polytheists, they are aware that other people in other places consider someone else to be God; monotheists only differ from polytheists in that the latter, unlike the former, are not disturbed by this circumstance (homage paid to one god in no way interferes, for them, with the homage paid to another one: it does not betray the one or the other). When speaking of religions, belief in a higher power plays the role of a *genus proximum*, while belief in the 'uniqueness' of one being chosen among many, coupled with the conviction that the others are therefore false usurpers, is the *differentia specifica* of monotheism. The awareness of more than one pretender to the name of God not only does *not* conflict with a monotheistic stance, but actually justifies it and, one might say, gives it flesh. If Adonai were the only contender (if all the neighbours of the Israelites worshipped in the same temple as they did), then what would the qualifier 'one and only' be for?! In your formulation – that the 'alleged followers of monotheism...fight so virulently against those who do not share their beliefs' – I believe the first word to be incorrect and misleading. They are most certainly true, bona fide followers – not merely 'alleged' monotheists – when (and because) they are doing it. But I have other reservations about the quote from Veyne: how could the 'myths of polytheism' create a 'desire to praise God as monarch'? As for the 'myths of Islam', we could use its variety of monotheism to explain Mohammed and the Caliphs' desire for domination – but the Roman Empire, similarly greedy for power, easily reconciled its lust for domination with an official policy of polytheism. That is, until monotheistic Rome's war against heretics and those of other faiths led to its fall.

Furthermore, the future and alternatives...you write: 'If people [I assume you mean humanity as a whole, which today is divided into countless churches] could agree upon the existence of a Single and Transcendent God, this "mistaken" belief in tribal gods would merely be seen as one of many, similar to people's – after all, limited – postulations about the Unreachable and Inconceivable. But this way, by comparing their own ideas to those of others, they are ready to fight, and not just to first blood, but without stopping until they destroy their adversary.' You advocate for a universal monistic faith, though not a unified liturgy. It is a beautiful vision, and I would gladly sign on to it, except that, considering the many functions in which that faith is entangled, it looks to me as one of the least realistic scenarios. Ultimately, as Fredrik Barth, one of the wisest anthropologists, proved in the last century, boundaries are not drawn in order to certify differences; differences are sought because boundaries are drawn.

In the face of a multiplicity of faiths and animosities between them of varying degrees of aggressiveness, one can count on two different strategies for mitigating the harms they cause to human co-existence and to the chances of improving it. One of them is the stance you imply: that God is one, and many are the ways to sing His praises. This strategy is not without its advantages: the possibility of limiting battles 'to first blood' is among them – but not the guarantee of self-constraint. In a more distant perspective, though not quite light-years away and to be ignored at our peril, lies in wait the spectre of totalitarianism (in another context, with a different vocabulary but a similar semantic field, Karl Jaspers was terrified by the idea of a global government because in its case there would be nowhere to escape or to hide). Why would the battle stop at first blood? Where is the limit to *casus belli*, the transgressions that can be spied out in canons of faith and the pragmatics of the liturgy? After all, this strategy derives its logic and sense from the axioms of a totalitarian system of order – that is, from the idea of the sinfulness of everything that differs and from the presumption of its guilt until it proves to be 'toeing the line' or repents its errors. Heterodoxy itself, by reason of being heterodox, is cast a priori on the defendant's bench. But there is also another strategy, which sees diversity not as a flaw but as a virtue, and even goes as far as saying that a successful and mutually beneficial co-existence, with expanded horizons and enriched experiences, is possible *because* (and not *in spite*!) of the diversity of the ways of life. Everyone here has, to use a religious idiom, the right to possess their own God, as long as the rights of one do not intrude upon the rights of another, or require refusing or depriving the other of that right. This is something akin to the 'constitutional patriotism' of Jürgen Habermas, which does not collide with the right to a cultural self-identity (ethnicity, language, customs), but provides in fact its most reliable and trustworthy protection.

We see again eye to eye when you object to a frivolous or even nihilistic thesis – that, seemingly, these 'differences aren't meaningful and that everything becomes liquid or changes colours based on context and the experience of the here and now'. In voicing this objection, Levinas would be your ally. Differences do make a difference – and for this reason they are significant, and so it does matter what kind of differences they are. This comes with a proviso that each difference may seek its expression in an idiom of its own (and so we are inclined to express them in differing idioms, without playing down their alterity, but emphasizing their different aspects). But I do not think that Levinas viewed salvation inside the self rather than in an encounter with the Other (he believed each such encounter to be giving birth to morality). In my understanding, his reflections quoted here refer to what the temptation tempts us with: and it tempts precisely by being a moment of freedom – the moment between opening one door and closing another. Life without temptation would be one of servitude – a routine with no prospects, a standstill, an inert environment, and one's own impotence and haplessness. Life after surrender to temptation is also a life of servitude – though we have yet to arrive at that truth, and typically we attain this wisdom after the damage is done. Only the state of temptation is a moment – a brief one, easy to overlook or misinterpret – of freedom: the possibility of a choice is still live, the door is still open. The die is not yet cast, but in the next instant, once I succumb to the temptation, it will be. I read Levinas' reflections as a warning: temptation is the artful, albeit treacherous, gimmick of Thanatos; it deploys the charms of freedom to ensnare. Be careful! Freedom could be slavery's bait (much like the road to hell that is paved with good intentions) and, if you are not mindful, you will fail to notice the prison ahead before you cross the threshold and hear the sound of the doors slamming behind you.

But I resorted to these reflections of Levinas to point out that God's invitation addressed to humanity – an invitation to participate in completing the act of creation by rendering the world moral – is manifested by the gift of free will, with all its benefits and all its snares.

SO   Well then, we will continue to argue, although it is not argument that is the goal here, but reaching that one, single, truth that emerges from battle. Maybe its allure is not based on its singularity, but on its unattainability? So we can continue clarifying, disputing for eternity? In any case I must begin by expressing contrition for my overly cavalier reference to a rather severe judgment on the history of Imperial Rome, which somewhat sourly assessed the pretentions of monotheists. That said, I would nonetheless defend it, while simultaneously acknowledging you, Zygmunt, as correct. How? I will begin by saying that you are absolutely correct, that monotheism does not necessarily exclude the possibility of the existence of other gods – rather, as you rightfully point out, its very raison d'être is to fight against them. So I absolutely agree with you, that monotheism's structure is fundamentally agonistic – and that it derives both its reason for being and its strength from conflict. But I am also willing to agree with Veyne, because within his sceptical approach to monotheism lurks what is actually a suspicion (that I am ready to share) of the existence of other, far more threatening forms of polytheistic religion.

How does this happen? Consider whether believers in one true God truly believe in one God, or rather pay homage to their own, localized ways of imagining Him. It is precisely in this sense that I agree with Veyne's 'alleged' monotheism, which is more threatening than polytheism because it conceals its true face, and because of its lack of the sympathetic features of an inclusive religion that can without difficulty pay homage to various gods. You say that my idea of paying tribute to one God in various forms is utopian. Agreed, but aren't utopias a measure of changes that took place once upon a time and might even be happening before our very eyes? I truly believe this. The real problem with believers in monotheism is based on the fact that, on the one hand, they tolerate differences (everyone who believes in 'my God' becomes my brother or sister), but, on the other, they build new walls. And those walls cannot be crumbled – once I have possessed this one single truth, why should I keep searching? The only thing left to do is to announce it to others, and, if the occasion presents itself, to force them to believe in it. To possess the truth is so all-consuming that the walls built around it can only be stronger, higher, simply unconquerable. Dialogue and interaction become not only unnecessary, but even redundant, interfering with the bliss of the possessed truth. The only thing that remains is conversion, opening the eyes, and in extreme circumstances excluding or even killing the adversary. This is my main objection, Zygmunt, to followers of monotheism.

But I did not forget. I myself am a believer in one God – I am after all a Christian, even a Roman Catholic. So I am really writing about my own trespasses. My only defence is that for many years I have been trying to overcome the burdens of this past. I do not want to convert or exclude anyone. Quite the opposite; as you noticed, I am drawn to diversity and multiplicity, because in it I see the possibility of overcoming the temptation that I, as a believer in one God, succumbed to for far too long. It is helpful here to recall the distinction delineated by Fredrik Barth, whom I once, thanks to you, very much enjoyed reading. Of course he is correct when he says that boundaries once drawn occasionally become a source of heated argument, and are always doomed to failure by the fluidity of life, the search for differences. And this is not only in religion, after all (though in it the phenomenon of the neophyte is particularly noticeable: those who can, with a zeal worthy of a greater cause, throw aside their old beliefs and passionately defend new ones). As it seems to me, in our newly minted democracies we can also see this in cases of so-called 'historical politics'. In vain did the brilliant, recently deceased Slavicist Maria

Bobrownicka warn Slavs against the 'drug of the myth' of national Romantic illusions. They blossom, not only in the effusions of prophets, but more broadly in the entire nation, as myths of innocence. These reborn champions of historical politics strive to persuade even me that only we Poles have passed the test of history, that our Polish deeds are singular and unrepeatable. I suspect, however, that similar trials were endured by Lithuanians and Ukranians and Russians and Slovaks, not to mention the court historians of Belarusian dictators. I have students from all of these countries, and sometimes also from places as distant as Spain, Turkey and China, and all of them have their own histories, just as unrepeatable and singular, to tell. This polyphony in no way becomes a cacophony; it takes the form of a subtle commentary on things beyond the imagination of historians, especially of political pundits.

And, finally, I want to return to Levinas and the problem of temptation you raised. I have to admit that I read him overly literally, and probably one-sidedly and unfairly. If the Other teaches me to understand what morality is, then of course I cannot speak here of being closed or cut off from other people. The only thing that remains is openness and the risks of the encounter undertaken. Maybe it's a problem of semantics. Maybe I am overly eager to avoid temptation because I associate it with evil and sin? So I have to think about this and search my conscience. It is probably my Catholic background that has trained me to run from temptation like the devil from holy water, without inquiring whether it may hold the seeds of understanding. Meanwhile, in Levinas – and in you, Zygmunt – I find an eloquent advocate for the claim that entertaining temptation is important, perhaps even constitutive of morality, and thus of the quality of human-ness. And if so, then of course I will agree to undertake it – I will give myself up to temptation because it heralds the new and the unknown. Moreover, to recall the end of your statement, 'God's invitation addressed to humanity – an invitation to participate in completing the act of creation by rendering the world moral – is manifested by the gift of free will, with all its benefits and all its snares.' If we call temptation God's invitation, then only a fool would not accept it.

ZB Dear Staszek, contention is probably the main temptation that inspired Levinas to think of the divine provenance of temptations, and me to endorse his hypothesis. But as to my (and I suspect Levinas') motives, it is not the prospect of a single truth that inclined me to rehabilitate contention, but precisely the moment of suspension, an instant of un-finishedness, under-definition, non-determination, a glimmer of freedom in the fissure in a cowed existence, when nothing has yet been decided for certain and seemingly everything – and if not everything, then at least an infinite lot of things – is still possible, so there is a chance for the epiphany of responsibility which at other times is hidden cravenly behind the mask of necessity.

Of course you are right when you remark that the horizon of contestation is 'one truth' (as a matter of fact, a truth without a qualifier – the sole truth worthy of its name); but, considering the agonistic pedigree of truth, I would praise that contestation for conceiving the temptation of truth (giving a concrete destination to a journey that without it would degrade into an aimless drifting), rather than for its potential for fulfilment. Contest is the domain of 'in order to', beset on both sides by the persistence of 'because of'. One would like to say, as did Goethe's Faust, 'Werd ich zum Augenblicke sagen: Verweile doch! Du bist so schön!' ('If I'd say to the moment: Abide, you are so fair') – but the punishment for such a desire, as Goethe warned us, is hellfire.[6] As for us, seasoned veterans of the twentieth century that we are, we might be tempted to point to, instead of hellfire, the camps. To the question asked by an inmate of Auschwitz about the reason for yet another unprovoked cruelty to yet another prisoner, the Kapo from Primo Levi's *Survival in Auschwitz* yelled, 'Hier ist kein warum!'[7]

Maurice Blanchot expressed a similar apprehension when saying that the reply is the curse of the question. Not being a poet but a craftsman of sociological prose, I would say simply: there is as much freedom as there is contention. And, as someone striving to be a moral being, I would add: there is as much responsibility as there is freedom. As to your question, 'Maybe its [truth's] allure is not based on its singularity, but on its unattainability?', I would answer: in that first allure inheres the temptation's snare; in the second, the chance of redemption.

It does not grieve or worry me, therefore, that, as you say, 'we will continue to argue'. If anything, my one concern is rather that we will run out of things to argue about. And this fear is not groundless, as increasingly a consensual vision is emerging from our polemics, except that we are painting it using slightly different palettes. For example, when you point out that the problem with monotheists' influence on human development is that 'on the one hand, they tolerate differences (everyone who believes in "my God" becomes my brother or sister), but, on the other, they build new walls', it grieves me that in my inventory of monotheism's properties, I omitted this issue. Of course, you are correct. There isn't a shadow of disagreement between us here, and so no cause for contestation.

Robert D. Putnam, a hugely influential political scientist, introduced and popularized the idea, now widely accepted and deployed throughout the social sciences, of 'social capital' – the density and durability of social ties and mutual trust as the yarn used by human individuals in weaving and padding what we might call their 'social nests', with the quality of that yarn determining both the density and the durability of the social fabric.[8] Putnam differentiates between two kinds of social capital: 'bridging' and 'bonding' – though in my opinion he is describing (and if he isn't, he should be!) not two *types of capital*, but two *modes of its utilization* – or two *goals* for which that capital can be, and tends to be, used. 'Bridging' uses of social capital are visible in the efforts of social advancement (and the reverse, its lack of bridging, is manifested in social degradation), whereas, in the case of 'bonding', capital is used to cement groups and entrench oneself in inherited or attained positions (for instance, by limiting outsiders' access to the group, excluding intruders or limiting the right to free choice accorded to the group's members). What in Putnam's theory is most relevant to our subject matter is the universality (ubiquity?) of social capital as the building block of social organization, but also the versatility of its uses. The co-presence of companions or brothers-in-arms, cemented by a trust in mutual loyalty and minimizing the risk of apostasy, is just as crucial for throwing the gates invitingly open as it is for digging moats, raising drawbridges and building ramparts – and indeed it is used for both goals. Bah! I would say that these two opposite goals are like heads and tails – no coin can ever do without both. Social capital, which we all possess though in unequal measure, is a powerful sword – but it is important to remember that the characteristic of all swords is to cut both ways. Not only monotheistic churches, but all social groups arise and derive their capacity of survival from a dialectic of integration and separation, amalgamation and alienation, inclusion and exclusion, opening and closing. The proportions of these opposing processes, intertwined in any act of group formation, as well as the proportion of attention given to one or the other, may be different in different circumstances, but neither of the two processes can be entirely eliminated. They are present, even if in various doses and intensities, in the existence of criminal gangs and in Médecins Sans Frontières. This is something like the case of the dialectics of safety and freedom with which I attempted to grapple on so many occasions: it is hard for them to co-exist, but they cannot get by without each other. Our human world is so arranged, and we are situated in it in such a way, that we are capable of living without both no more than one-handed people are capable of clapping.

It is with such an ambivalent weapon in our hands that it falls to us to fulfil our vocation of completing the act of creation. We do not have any other weapon, and so the dual potency of our armament is unavoidable. I do not think that we will ever desist from following the urge to convert and/or to exclude: both inclinations are inevitable and inescapable ingredients of our human way of being-in-the-world; it is for that reason, among others, that we are burdened with the task of making the world moral – and this is why the ultimate fulfilment of our vocation, the completion of creation, is postponed for eternity.

Inviting us to assist in paving the road to goodness and closing it to evil, God did not promise us an easy life. He only announced to Adam that he would earn his bread by the sweat of his brow, and to Eve that in labour she shall bear her children.

SO You are expressing a serious concern that we will run out of things to argue about. I am not worried about it. Despite the affinities that I perceive, with great satisfaction, between your way of looking at the world, Zygmunt, and mine, I nonetheless still see differences, which make those affinities all the more interesting. Let's argue a little more about Levinas, who is so close to you, and who is after all not so far from me. Nonetheless, when you say that action as such is an action hardly intended, an unachieved state in which 'a glimmer of freedom [appears] in the fissure in a cowed existence', then I am a little bit afraid of this glimmer. Of course if I am dealing with a person who has a finely honed sense of morality, and who perceives in the epiphany of an Other, as Levinas does, that 'The epiphany of the other person is *ipso facto* my responsibility toward him',[9] then I am in full agreement. But if the Other appears to be dangerous, or as a victim to be exploited, then what is to be done with the glimmer of that possibility? I am missing the conclusion, calling things by their names, defining clear conditions and setting boundaries. Because, after all, experience teaches us that not every encounter is, as you describe it, 'a chance for the epiphany of responsibility'. I say all this in order to persuade you that we will not run out of material for conflict.

I was very drawn to what you wrote about Robert D. Putnam. But Putnam does not only write about the dual meaning of 'social capital'. It seems to me that his analyses are so persuasive to us because he was the first to point out the erosion and dilution of social belief. He was the first to notice that Americans of his generation preferred 'bowling alone' – to recall the title of his book – to participating in group entertainments that would strengthen and even cement that collective. You are right to emphasize that 'padding [the] "social nest"' brought people closer, made the world familiar and home-like. And isn't it telling that the same Robert Putnam's new book *American Grace*, written with David Campbell in 2010, had a subtitle that both was very meaningful, and betrayed the helplessness of a devoutly believing person (as you know, Putnam converted to Judaism because he perceived a greater seriousness in the way Jews treated faith): 'How religion divides and unites us'.[10] The book is an astonishing record of the divisions and increasing tensions between people who are followers of the same faith. Thus, it is not only the believers of various monotheisms who are differing and dividing amongst themselves, as we discussed earlier, but Christians themselves who perceive each other with increasing hostility and distrust (the same can be said of the internal divisions among Jews and Muslims). The material collected by Robert Putnam and his collaborator is honestly depressing, and sheds new light on the consolatory statistics of those opposed to the secularization of American society's 'traditional religious nature'. One side accuses the other of excessive liberalism and being overly open to the so-called 'world' and its pleasures, and the other avenges itself by accusing its opponents of being fundamentalists and fanatics.

How are we to explain this? Why are the ties between people, which had been so painstakingly constructed, being frayed and severed by the same hands, and using the same arguments (fidelity to tradition, and interpretation of it that is both correct and in accordance with God's will) that created them? I narrow my focus. I look at our Polish quarrels and increasing polarization. I do not find any explanation for them. It puzzles me more and more. I will not conceal the fact that, after our exchange of observations of the same world from different perspectives, you really hit on something when you described yourself as a 'craftsman of socio-logical prose. Your craft, Zygmunt, very much intrigues me. I am even of the opinion that you can perceive far more than I, as I grapple with the plenitude of theological literature, outside of which I am less and less able to perceive the human. But sometimes I have the sense that it doesn't even have that much in common with God. This was made clear to me recently by Ulrich Beck, whose book (*A God of One's Own*) I have been perusing on your recommendation, and I am astonished by his acuity in describing a reality heretofore reserved for theologians. Is it time for sociologists to offer their spiritual sensitivity to theologians and scholars of religion, and open their/our eyes to the world of God?

I don't know whether this is a provocation, or a call made out of humility and an inability to experience the world I live in.

ZB You write, Staszek, 'I am a little bit afraid of this glimmer'...I share your fear – except that it is not a little fear in my case – I am very seriously afraid and concerned! But after a moment's reflection on this fear and trembling, I stop, because in the last account they prove better than any alternative. This game is worth all the world's candles!

The tree in Eden was the Tree of the Knowledge of Good *and* Evil – named in one breath, because, in isolation from each other, individually, neither the one nor the other would make any sense. Before tasting the fruit, Adam and Eve did not know that they were naked. In the world of paradise blessed with primordial harmony, there was no room for error, and thus for fear of error. But neither was there room for the idea of good (note that the sixth day of Creation was the only one *not* summarized by God with the 'it was good' sentence, so leaving the matter open – for humankind). That first couple lived in daily contact with God and could, if asked, give the same answer that God would give many years later to Moses' question – but after eating the apple they could no longer do so: they knew that there is good and that there is evil, and that one has to choose between the two; and if there is a choice, there must be a possibility of error, and so also uncertainty. The moment that *uncertainty* was born was the moment that *morality* was born – together with the moral *self*, a self aware of walking a tightrope. That awareness insured the paradise against the return of the exiled couple and their offspring more effectively than cherubs and swirling swords! An ethical code with rules for making right choices would not help the exiles from the paradise of unequivocality (freedom from alternatives); every *rule* assumes that there is a possibility of behaving differently (otherwise why have rules?!) – assuming therefore the presence of temptations – and it is precisely thanks to the presence of these that the moral self can come to be. The temptation of temptation consists in the temptation to be moral – to choose good and reject evil. Might it lead them into the wilderness? But there was no wilderness in paradise! And so on, ad infinitum. Morality is not a recipe for an easy (read: worry-free, tranquil) life. It would not be morality, were it such a recipe. Sentencing them to choosing, and thus exposing them to the temptation of temptation, God invited humans to participate in the act of creation. And in creation as in creation's nature (and, generally speaking, as in the nature of all freedoms): it will not happen without 'dangers' or 'sacrifices to be made'. As our neighbours from beyond our eastern border say: 'volkov bojat'sia, w les nie chodit' (If you are afraid of wolves, don't walk into the forest).

As for the lonely bowlers – in the workplace, in neighbourhoods, in the family circle, and all around, even in the places we go when seeking an escape from loneliness, namely, inside the online 'social networks': our world is less and less hospitable to solidarity. The world divided into communities – 'social bodies' – was a factory of solidarity. Dividing the inhabited world into 'individuals' burdened with the responsibility of self-determination and self-affirmation in a context of fragile social ties and a lack of norms, is on the contrary a factory of mutual suspicion and competition. It devalues all coalitions except ad hoc ones, and all shared activities except those aimed at specific short-term tasks. The result is life lived on a minefield or quicksand, generating a constant, massive nostalgia for clear maps and signposts engraved in rock; for a leash, a muzzle and shackles – as well as for a leader imbued with power to command and imputed with infallibility, thereby liberating all followers from the hateful burden of individual responsibility. This is not a new phenomenon – Erich Fromm, and soon after him Christopher Lash, have already provided colourful and detailed descriptions of the mechanism and dynamics of the 'escape from freedom' – but the feeling of aimlessness, loneliness, and the threat of abandonment or banishment was never as strong as it is now, and the nostalgia for 'pre-uncertainty', for a less shaky world, has never been so overwhelming: the temptation of 'voluntary servitude' was never as hard to resist as it is today. Let us not blame religious beliefs or churches for this situation. Nomadic yearnings and dreams feverishly, though blindly, seek a haven in which to anchor, and so there will be no shortage of moorings on offer – varying in baits but strikingly similar in their promises – as long as the need for them does not dry up. Secular or religious versions of fundamentalism thrive in the same soil; religious or political sects and/or market corporations prey upon the same awareness of one's own insufficiency haunting the *Mann ohne Verwandschaften* – the man without bonds.

SO   So, I will begin from the end. You say, Zygmunt, that the breeding grounds of fundamentalisms, whether they be secular or religious, are the same – man's longing for signs, certainties, which he does not find in himself, and therefore seeks, longingly searching for solutions, experts, authorities. This is true. I observe its accuracy even when reading the results of the Gallup study, which as usual encompasses the entire globe. Referring to self-identification or declared affiliations, they examine fluctuations and changes among the religious community and those who call themselves atheists. They generate understandable interest. The faithful feel confirmed in the correctness of their beliefs, and atheists track the rise of rational convictions in the world's inhabitants with high hopes. In Poland, both of these feelings are shared by Poles, though the number of believers is decidedly in the majority. I personally do not attach great weight to these measurements, as I am far more interested in the quality of those convictions, be they religious or atheist. That is what decides the quality of the co-existence of these groups. And this is not looking so good, as within both groups I observe a kind of polarization and the growth of fundamentalist tendencies, which do not bode well for either religion or atheism. As I see it, both groups make strong, and in my view controversial – or even dubious – claims, which could not be confirmed or denied in an intellectual way. For one group, religious experience, and thus also faith in God, has a universal character and transcends cultural boundaries. But that same universality is called into question by the very real existence of non-believers (whose numbers grow rather than decreasing). For the second group, it is the rationality of the world, existing without religious references, which testifies to a mature insight into the essence of things. This belief likewise seems to transcend cultural boundaries, because one finds it everywhere. It is worthwhile to recall the sober and perceptive observation of the late-lamented Leszek Kołakowski that 'belief is valid and disbelief is valid and both are necessary to culture', and that what is most important is the creative tension between these two positions.[11] And here I would like to address your crucial observation that 'The moment that *uncertainty* was born was the moment that *morality* was born – together with the moral *self*, a self aware of walking a tightrope.' In saying this, you also touch on my desire to rid myself of a fear of a glimpse of the unknown, which also contains various possibilities, including the possibility of choosing evil. This is an unpleasant discovery, but it is also somehow purifying.

I am formed of the same stuff as the majority (maybe all of?) the world's inhabitants. That is our shared *conditio humana* and there is no reason to pretend that it is otherwise. Maybe an awareness of this shared fate would decrease tensions and the polarizations between people, particularly in Poland, but probably also in other countries as well. Here I am interested, despite everything, in the insights of sociologists of religion, who perceive interesting interdependencies. I am thinking of the conclusions stemming from the in-depth research of Professor Józef Baniak and the careful estimates of Professor Janusz Mariański, both Polish sociologists of religion and authors of many publications in Polish, unfortunately till now not translated into English. From their findings, it emerges that the growing religious scepticism of Poles, particularly of the younger generation, is closely tied to the qualitative offerings of the Catholic Church in our country. In particular, we can observe a growing resentment among school-children and university students who were subjected to so-called 'religious education' in school, or more precisely, to a rather unconvincing indoctrination in the Catholic catechism. I observe a similar interconnection with the political engagement of the Catholic hierarchy. Weren't we also able to observe similar links during a time period that is rightly – and, let us hope, definitively – past, when the atheistic indoctrination in Communist Poland failed? Any large-scale efforts to confirm it were met with growing resistance.

What then are we to do, how are we to avoid extinguishing the flickering flame of moral revelation born out of fundamental uncertainty? I really do not know. The one thing that comes to my mind is to remind each other of the necessity of being sensitive to and wary of the excessive certainty that comes from a feeling of power. And given that power is usually illusory, its possessors typically recognize this too late...

III

The Literati in Aid of
Blundering Thought

Zygmunt Bauman So we return to our starting point, to Kołakowski's contention that God is an acknowledgment of humankind's inadequacy. 'Believers' are aware of this inadequacy (eternal, incurable), whereas atheists (as well as – though surreptitiously, stealthily – agnostics, who suspect that atheists are right, but are not bold enough to make their suspicions public, or follow Pascal's wager) deny this human inadequacy, or acknowledge it only conditionally, seeing it as a temporary problem that will not persist past mankind's domination of the cosmos. Both groups assemble a totality from a painfully incomplete image of the world and the human condition; they do it in seemingly opposite ways, but with similar results for dialogue, not to mention mutual understanding: once their image of the world is complete (or rather 'made sensible' thanks to this act of assemblage), then pricking up one's ears to hear an opinion that won't fit into that image is a sheer waste of time – or even an act of betrayal. Listening to the things that do reach those ears would completely undo the spiritual peace that was so laboriously acquired. The 'inadequacy' I am discussing here has two faces: ignorance and impotence. Ignorance: this is what the human mind cannot grasp, but there must be some logic in it, it's just that it is not of the kind that the human mind could comprehend – *credo quia absurdum*. And impotence – these forces can never be conquered by humans, they will never be made predictable and obedient to human will: humans shoot, but a being more-than-human – God – directs the bullet...

This inadequacy also has two settings: social and individual. The first assisted in the birth of Enlightenment rationalism, born out of an opposition to the idea that the human species, no matter how skilfully it made use of its two strong arms, reason and technology, could never fully know the world or rake it under its control. In our era of individualism, we have abandoned the idea of a perfectly knowledgeable 'human species'. Instead, it is the individual variant of inadequacy that depresses us. The world is inconceivable and ungovernable not only *in spite of*, but *as a result of* human actions: even I, personally, am ignorant and impotent in relation to *their* (other people's) intentions and actions. Too much (social) evil for fighting it on one's own. During the years of the First World War, the Germans inscribed 'Gott mit uns' (God be with us) on soldiers' belts. During the last Olympics, countless runners, individually, were fervently crossing themselves before the start. They asked their 'individual God' to rob their neighbours to the left and the right of their advantages and so deny them victory.

The dilemma emerging from this was beautifully (far more beautifully than I could do it) presented by J. M. Coetzee. Allow me to quote him at length:

> I have no desire to associate myself with the people behind the Intelligent Design Movement. Nevertheless, I continue to find evolution by random mutation and natural selection not just unconvincing but preposterous as an account of how complex organisms came into being. As long as there is not one of us who has the faintest idea how to go about constructing a housefly from scratch, how can we disparage as intellectually naïve the conclusion that the housefly must have been put together by an intelligence of a higher order than our own? If anyone in the picture is naïve, it is the person who elevates the operating rules of Western science into epistemological axioms, arguing that what cannot be demonstrated scientifically to be true (or, to use the more timid word preferred by science, *valid*), cannot be true (valid)...
>
> Why do we human beings typically experience awe – a recoil of the mind, as if before an abyss – when we try to comprehend, *grasp*, certain things, such as the origin of space and time, the being of nothingness, the nature of understanding itself? I cannot see what

evolutionary advantage this combination gives us – the combination of insufficiency of intellectual grasp together with consciousness that the grasp is insufficient.[1]

Ultimately Coetzee, relying on the findings of Eugène Marais (a South African naturalist and twentieth-century poet) comes to a resigned conclusion: 'an intellectual apparatus marked by a conscious knowledge of its insufficiency is an evolutionary aberration'.[2]

Well, what do you think, Staszek?

Stanisław Obirek John Maxwell Coetzee is a unique phenomenon and I am glad that you brought up his penetrating analysis of the very situation that we are discussing. On the one hand, he refers to sources of a dawning awareness (which seems to be the criterion for separating us from other creatures, because even here there is no certainty!), and on the other, he indicates dangerous possibilities lurking in the temptation to deify it. From this, as I understand it, comes his unconcealed distaste for 'the people behind the Intelligent Design Movement'. Coetzee is too skilled a wordsmith to take even a single one lightly. He says that it is not Intelligent Design that annoys him, but its efforts to convert people. He knows what he is saying. In an America that is enthralled by its own religiosity, it is these very pressures that create a hell on earth for all who express their doubts about the project. However, fans of the witty Richard Dawkins cannot feel entirely safe either, because Coetzee has a bitter pill at hand for them as well. Even their theory will not withstand a sceptical gaze, particularly one supplemented with a commentary that is not entirely lacking in spite, as when Coetzee says that to him it seems 'not just unconvincing but preposterous'. In brief, this fragment of Coetzee's invites me to extend my uncertainty, even to dwell in it. I really enjoy the way that he writes about it – because he is merely alluding to it. And in this discretion I discern his incredible talent and far-sightedness. This kind of approach evades all attempts at definitive answers about the origins of our world, its development and continuation. It is also a pointed and radical confrontation with experts of all kinds, be they religious or atheist, who, with the zeal of a higher cause, serve up such definitive answers to their followers.

Zygmunt, you write about this with a lucidity rivalling Coetzee's, pointing to the passion for collecting proofs, which it is so hard to retreat from and which growing masses of followers flock to. Isn't Intelligent Design, or a makeshift theory constructed for the purposes of an equally makeshift ideology, an a-priori accepted thesis that would allow for vanquishing 'heretics'? And doesn't the evolutionary model – so masterfully developed by the already-mentioned Dawkins in his numerous publications – serve his aco-lytes (presumably not himself) in mocking 'idiots', and hasn't it become a proverbial flail that restricts any reflection on the origins of life and consciousness? In brief, it seems to me that literature is becoming a useful medium for naming that,which is also evoked in our conversation, – namely, the unknown. Henryk Markiewicz from Jagiellonian University, who was my teacher of literary theory, called literature the solution of ideology. I think it is a very accurate metaphor, and indicates the utilitarian function of litera-ture. I do not see it as demeaning to writers, but rather as an expression of respect and an acknowledgment of their social value. The lessons of the book that you took the fragment from are still before me, but that fragment serves as a kind of lens that brings into focus the problems, whose solutions created so many difficul-ties for the architects of modernity, and continue to torment us. Didn't the *cogito ergo sum* that so dazzled Descartes become a source of scepticism for Spinoza, who found an answer (so bitter to his contemporaries) in *deus sive natura*. Meanwhile, neither my own subjectivity, nor divine nature, give me any rest. I also do not find it in the ideas of Eugène Marais referenced by Coetzee. So what remains? Despair, resignation. I don't want to believe it. Maybe you can suggest something, Zygmunt? Do you have a source of hope that you would like to write to me about?

ZB   I will summon another author to my rescue: this time Günther Anders. He coined the notion of the 'Prometheus syndrome'. The manifestation of this syndrome is that we are equally tormented by the excellence of the things which we *find* and the things which we *make*: both the first and the second set the bar at heights we are incapable of jumping (things we find, such as the housefly mentioned by Coetzee, too ingeniously constructed for us to replicate, and things we make, such as guided missiles or comput-ers, which by far surpass us – frail and hapless creatures as we are – with their destructive force or with the exquisitely dependable monotony of their precision); and all that despite the fact that for centuries we have been trying to equal them as hard as we can – and, yet more often, as we cannot.

Promethean syndrome mixes Promethean shame with Promethean jealousy: we are ashamed of our inferiority, but also filled with an overpowering urge to escape it and attain equality with – or, better yet, superiority over – the machines. Hundreds of thousands of researchers in countless laboratories investigate processes that lead Nature (which is *deus sive...*) to produce a fly's feet, but then again Lieutenant Calley's soldiers could not resist the temptation to land their helicopters in the village of May Lai and do with their own hands what was done with such shameful, humbling efficiency by cutting-edge machine guns and napalm bombs.

Beside the fear of the unknown and refractory, Promethean syndrome also makes out of inadequacy – of both thought and action, of understanding and the action potential – an intolerable state, simultaneously alienating and humiliating. And as the prospect of both the social and the individual inadequacy being overcome in a foreseeable future is highly unlikely, there is also little hope that we will ever rid ourselves of it, much as of fear. There is no lack of evidence for the fact that this syndrome is an inseparable attribute of the human condition. What, then, is left for us? Only to learn to reconcile ourselves to its tiresome company. We could at best mitigate its more harmful aspects – by becoming comfortable with inadequacy, which would remove the venom of its sting. That, in my reading, is what Coetzee suggests: let us reconcile ourselves to being an aberration of evolution – and to the premonition that we will never cease to be one; that there are accomplishments that we will never achieve by our own industry. That, in brief, regardless of whether or not God exists, we are not gods and stand no chance of becoming them.

Neither of the two would actually require such a great sacrifice. Because the things we would have left to think about and to do after becoming reconciled to our own limitations would more than suffice for keeping countless generations of people busy: for instance, facing up to the intellectual and material challenges we must deal with in order for those countless generations to be.

SO These suggestions from writers are intriguing, forcing us to rethink things that had seemed familiar, even obvious – for example, as with Günther Anders' 'Promethean syndrome'. A psychiatrist friend of mine used to say that psychiatrists and priests suffer from the same sickness – 'messiah syndrome'; we not only want to save people, but also are convinced that we are doing. The results, for the patients and penitents trusting in our care, are often disastrous. Although I have not been 'priesting' since 2005, and have thus been less pestered by the messianic temptation, I know how overpowering it can be. I return to Anders and his poignant analysis of the paradoxical relationship man has to the objects he creates. Not only have they torn themselves away from their maker, they have assumed a monstrous form and conquered him, evoking feelings of shame and mortification. I've encountered a similar diagnosis in the works of Stanisław Lem, especially in his *Summa technologiae*, which astonishes with the breadth of its perspective. This association is especially apropos, because Anders considered Lem to be one of the few authentic philosophers of the technological age. I must therefore return to Anders' *Die Antiquiertheit des Menschen* ('The Antiquatedness of Mankind') (I cannot understand why this still awaits a Polish translation; it ought to be required reading for anyone who wants to understand the world we live in)[3] in order to grasp the essence of Gunther Anders' 'Promethean syndrome'. For now I am left with the memory of unfinished conversations with Stanisław Lem, which were very moving to me at the time, and which I still come back to with a sense of amazement at his brilliance and rare sensitivity. I have written about them many times, but I would like to draw on them for the purposes of our conversation.

Moved by the moral anxieties of Lem, I asked him where his great care for the world and for people came from. After all, I said stupidly, this is the domain of believers, 'servants of God', not atheists like him, who are indifferent to the moral condition of humankind. I was a priest at the time and among those who ostensibly cared about morality, as it were. As you can imagine, Lem defeated me with a shrug of his shoulders, remarking caustically that it was the position of careless thoughtlessness that he found surprising and that seemed incomprehensible to him, particularly among priests and people *ex professo* involved with morality, above all among believers concerned by the declining numbers of people willing to share their religious passions. I think that Anders' reaction would be similar; from what I remember, in one of the final interviews before his death, he said that, to the repeated accusation that he was irresponsibly lacking in hope, he replied that he believed this was always better than encouraging hopes in an equally irresponsible way. He was referring to the philosopher Ernst Bloch, whom he could not forgive for the irresponsible way he fed a hope that he could neither defend nor justify. I am not sure, Zygmunt, but I think that, by directing my attention to Günther Anders' 'Promethean syndrome', you seem to be suggesting that resigning from hope and other metaphysical supports allows one to gain an acuity of vision when looking at the surrounding world. This is what I think, and I return once more to the aforementioned conversation with Stanisław Lem (tragically ended by his unexpected sudden death in the Spring of 2006). When I confessed that his atheism, so attractively expressed in his books, exerted an irresistible allure that I was unable to repel, he practically shouted with horror – 'God forbid that I would deprive anyone of their faith!' It was this horror that made me understand how authentic his atheism was, and how problematic my own faith. It was an experience so profound that I constantly return to it, and every time I am in Kraków I hurry to Lem's grave at the Salwatorian Cemetery, to ask how things really are.

In any case, as you can see, I associate everything with faith and atheism, though at this point I am aware that neither one nor the other is the most important thing at this time. The point is rather what we do with the things we have created with our own hands and minds (after all, atheism and faith also belong to that order of things). And it is probably the palpable and verifiable results of the choices that we make, which emerge from our worldview, that attest to their truth and authenticity. And in that regard, things are not so great. Actually, they are getting worse. I have a feeling – and you have written about this many times – that mankind is managing itself ever worse, and the Promethean shame of Günther Anders is gradually becoming transmuted into an overly human fault. As one of Anders' students, Jean-Paul Sartre, wrote – we are becoming hell to each other. Is there a place where we could escape from the imminent apocalypse? I find increasingly little hope in myself; outside myself, even less. So maybe all that remains, as you suggest, is a calm acceptance of reality as it is, attempting to retain at the same time a spiritual calm. It isn't much, but tragic realism is still better than optimistic illusion.

Allow me, Zygmunt, to return once more to your books. From the time I met you (and that was in 2000 in Kraków when I succeeded in convincing you to write a piece for the Jesuit quarterly *Spiritual Life*'on the subject 'What Do Non-believers Believe In?') I have never stopped being amazed by the precision with which you react to everything that surrounds us and to what happens in the world. Meanwhile your commentaries are broadcast in every possible language, and listened to and read with great interest. It is enough to name the titles of your books from the last ten years to create a list of the most urgent problems of our times. What is even more interesting is that you not only diagnosed them, you also indicated sources, illuminated causes, and somewhat carefully suggested possible ideas for remedies. I admit that after reading them I was unable to think of those issues in any other way; your categories and ideas imposed themselves on me with a force that I could not – and did not want to – resist. It was the same with my students, many of whom decided to write a thesis that was based on your books. I do not want to make a list of these topics; it is enough to mention life on the fringe, people who are expendable, *Homo consumans*, the transformation of green pastures by global shepherds that today's worldwide concerns have become – shepherds for whom humans are the most cumbersome element of their profitable speculations – to get at the heart of your reflections. But of course you do not close your eyes to the consequences for the individual in today's global transformations. You are troubled by the participant in liquid reality who is constantly in pursuit of ever newer and stronger stimuli and is incapable of being content with what he has, is unable to take pleasure in the passing moment of his present life, but constantly chases illusions of the future, which escape all the faster, the more they are chased. And every more permanent attachment seems to preclude other, far more interesting possibilities, still unknown and therefore desired.

These analyses, which you do not shy away from in your many writings – and in the conversations which you do not refuse to Polish journalists – have led to us waiting for your opinion; we want to know what Zygmunt Bauman thinks of this or that. Simultaneously – something you are well aware of – your presence in the public sphere has contributed to your texts being adorned with somewhat unfavourable epithets declaimed by defenders of 'stable and unchanging values'. For them, you are a postmodernist (I am not sure if they know what that actually means), a nihilist, a demoralizer and destroyer of all values. What is more, you dare to touch sacred cows and mercilessly unveil the ideological lies of politicians, governments, even entire nations, which have the undeserved reputation of being defenders of democracy, resilient identity and the aforementioned stable and unchanging values. What do you think – where does it come from, this passion for attacking opinions and ideas that they don't even try to understand? We can forget about the trolls whose reason for existence is to fight against anyone with an opinion different from their own – I am thinking of potential allies, among whom I count rational people of faith. I count myself among them, and in your writing I find confirmations of my own intuitions, which you grasp far more precisely than I am able to. Do you have the feeling that you are acquiring allies, or that your analyses are also of interest to people of faith, and not only to dissatisfied activists on the Left? Something tells me that this is the case. And I found the proof a few years ago in Rome, in the Collegium Urbanum (which runs the missionary activities of the Catholic Church), where your books had a place of honour.

ZB Not being gods, especially Lev Shestov's god, who had the power to act retroactively and to make null and void – it never existed – the humanity-disgracing case of Athenian citizens treating Socrates to a bowl of hemlock, neither you nor I can undo our past. As you say, everything, to this very day, is associated for you with faith in God and atheism; for me, everything turns around the human title to humanity and the dangers of deifying humans. We both carry scars not fully healed – but in our youth we burned our fingers on somewhat different flames and have grown used to blowing on somewhat different burns: you on the enforcement of faith, me on the deification of man. We got our burns from bonfires kindled in apparently inimical camps: one of us in the camp of the Messiah, the other in the encampment of Prometheus; but in fact (as you will probably agree) both flames in both camps were lit on pyres built for the same heretic: *human limitations*. Blowing on singed fingers, you and I have reconciled ourselves, maybe, to our inadequacy, or at least are inclined to admit it (to understand, for example, that we will never know whether God exists or not – and accept that it is precisely that inability to find out, and the necessity to live with this awareness, on which humanity rests). Except that you are haunted by the desire to excuse yourself for such inadequacy – previously as sinful, now as a symptom of mental sluggishness; whereas I treat it not just as unavoidable, but as a part and parcel of the human condition.

But let me return to our joint topic. I do not know (and will never find out) who was the first of our ancestors to ask 'Why is there something instead of nothing?' But, once that question was asked, there was nothing that could be done to prevent the search for an answer. And we are still searching – being, as we are, members of a species of incurably curious creatures. For how many thousands of years, I have no idea; I suspect, however, that our descendants will devote no less time than their ancestors (including us) to the search for an answer. Because, no matter how precisely we measure the size of the universe, and the speed with which it expands, and how many dimensions we ascribe to it (we do eleven at the moment, but who will swear that there won't be more?!), and how many more nanoscopic elements, hadrons or whatever else we call them, are added to the units of energy and matter (or the 'dark matter' with which we strive to fill the gaps of knowledge in between all these things) – we will go on banging our heads against the same two limits that the human mind is incapable of crossing. Those limits are 'nothing' and 'infinity'. 'Cosmogony', a highly respectable field of scholarship funded lavishly for that reason, will add more details (and why wouldn't it?) to the description of the first nanoseconds after the Big Bang, and will never stop fidgeting between the eternal paradox of the creation of something out of nothing and the idea of eternal duration: the kind of challenge to which our minds, formed as they have been for servicing a finite life, are found to be grossly and sorely unequal, and which all the experience of our senses contradict. This is where the intellectual elements of human inadequacy, which our conversation is airing from all sides, have stalled for good.

God-the-Creator is the most attractive of the hypotheses offering an exit from this mental maze, because we include the inscrutability of His intentions and powers into the very concept of Him – not so much solving the paradox of 'something out of nothing', or intellectually grasping the ungraspable-because-infinite nature of time or space, as deriving some satisfaction and spiritual tranquillity from admitting our incapability of doing so. The opposite hypothesis, that something came from nothing of its own accord with no intervention from a higher power, is, after all, mentally ungraspable; true, it does not ask for a compromise and does not call the human mind to perform an inhuman feat of comprehending the incomprehensible, but puts before it a task which it is not fit to perform.

All this is, however, happening in a sphere different from that of human being-in-the-world – or, more simply, from the sphere of everyday reality. And returning to that everyday life scene, as a sociologist ought to, I assert that I follow neither Pangloss nor Dawkins; and, if pressed to express my opinion, I would repeat after Candide: 'il faut cultiver notre jardin' (Let's cultivate our garden). And I will do so without shame, and without any moral scruples. Because, as I keep repeating: the moral self is not made by commandments from on high, or by presumptions of reason, but from the indomitable fact of our dependence on other humans and on our solidarity. What is more, as you rightly suspect, I would add to my answer a quotation from Stanisław Lem: 'God forbid that I deprive anyone of their faith!' Except that I would do it without a sliver of horror, out of my trust in the human species' capability of bringing themselves to their senses.

As to the question of hope: if I did not have it, I would most probably not write books or give lectures. Why waste one's breath or use up one's pen, if there is no hope of being heard or read, and of that hearing or reading – possibly, though not necessarily – 'making a difference', even a little one (Rome wasn't built in a day). What humans have done, humans can undo. I do not accept that we have reached a point of no return: for the place in which we are now to become indeed a 'point of no return', we would need first to believe that it is already that, and is such irreversibly, once and for all. As long as a glimmer of hope blinks – even if from under a heap of ashes – we preclude such a possibility. As for myself, I would wish to play the role which in his time I accredited to Hłasko, being possessed as he was by the urge to warn: 'Look at yourselves, see how badly you behave and are doing; come to your senses, for God's and your own sake.' I fully agree with you that almost all signs on heaven and earth seem to be conspiring to refuse consolation to the troubled and the frightened – and if there is any hope for humanity, it resides in hope itself. While hope is still alive, writing obituaries for humanity is sorely premature. And I am unable to rid myself of the belief that hope is immortal; just like God, it can perish only together with humankind.

Man, Staszek dear, can,

IV

Sources of Hope

Stanisław Obirek Seeing as how I have succeeded in provoking a confession from you, let us discuss hope, and where we get it from. As I understand it, Zygmunt, for you philosophy (Voltaire and his *Candide*) and literature (Hłasko) remind us that *non omnis moriar* ('not all of me will die'), or, rather, that it is not worth living as if everything depended on us. Because even cultivating one's own garden, as Candide encourages us to do, and faith in the power of common sense, which Hłasko so strongly believed in, are precisely that. But it is not only texts that are important to us – at least not for me. I was very intrigued by your *excursus* on the consequences of contemplating why there tends to be something rather than nothing, or, rather, on the vast dimensions that modern-day cosmology opens up before us, which will make both those who believe in God, and atheists who are content with rational experiments, quite dizzy. I was reminded of children's dreams the first time I heard about the structure of an atom. I was fascinated, and I admit that it filled me with wonder: that every atom is like a galaxy, and the galaxy is like a large atom with its electrons, protons and neutrons; nowadays, one cannot even remember all the different particles within particles. Later I realized that these children's dreams were another variant of Kant's awe at the starry sky, which Ignatius Loyola also gazed at with fondness.

You rightfully made reference to the burns, which even years later serve as painful reminders. But they are not actually the most important thing to me. Instead, I remember specific faces, which to this day smile at me and say, 'Staszek, everything will be fine, even if you take a different path. And perhaps especially if you know why you are taking it.' Will you allow me to say a little more about this, counting on you to recall your own mentors who helped you on your way, either inviting you into Promethean faith or assisting you in walking away from its false promises? That's how it was in my case, but more on that in a moment.

In my understanding, faith in the power of the word, regardless of whether it is written or spoken, is what allows you to take on new, not at all Sisyphean, tasks. As you say, if not for the conviction that it does change something, that in spite of everything it is worthwhile to 'waste one's breath or use up one's pen' and take on more or less successful conversations with journalists – even though sometimes it results in things that the interviewee never expected – one would never do it. It would certainly be safer to write texts without journalistic additions, because, when doing so there is some hope that the improvised nature of the process will have a less deleterious effect on the thoughts and intentions of the author. The fact that you are constantly translated into new languages means that you are striking the right note, that you are giving names to things that others are only musing over. But I will give this a rest, I know that you do not enjoy discussing yourself; you much prefer to escape into ideas and the writing of others, such as Ulrich Beck or Richard Sennett, whom you enjoy referring to. But I am curious about the sources of your hope, though I also reach for the guides you indicate. I thought to myself that, if I told you about my guides, I might stir your memory. No, do not worry, this will not be a gallery of 'important people' or a reckoning of 'formative experiences' – more like a coming to terms with someone entering my life who had initially not seemed that important. Before I describe this, allow me, Zygmunt, a small quibble and disagreement with your differentiation, which you wisely weaken with the word 'apparently'. You say that 'We both carry scars not fully healed – but in our youth we burned our fingers on somewhat different flames and have grown used to blowing on somewhat different burns: you on the enforcement of faith, me on the deification of man. We got our burns from bonfires kindled in apparently inimical camps: one of us in the camp of the Messiah, the other in the encampment of Prometheus.' I will dare to say, that it is not really the 'Messiah' and 'Prometheus' that separate us, but our life experience, or concrete events or meetings that led us to make certain choices instead of others. I do not want to dwell on this, but I can easily imagine that if, in my teenage years in the seventies, I had encountered a fully convinced Party member who was able to persuade me of their beliefs, I would certainly have found myself in the Promethean camp rather than the messianic one. Because the very people who persuaded me to join institutionalized forms of religion were actually referencing (probably unknowingly) my disenchantment with academic, self-governing and government institutions, and that is why their alternatives appealed to me. It was, after all, similar in the case of that most important Messiah; he offered not a doctrine but a way of life ('come and see'), and in doing so relied on a human spark rather than a divine one.

After this perhaps overly lengthy and tiresome hedging, I come to the reason – Carlo Maria Martini. Yes, the very person about whom we heard so much after his death on 30 August 2012. I will not refer to the things that the media reported on with such enthusiasm (it is enough to refer to the short conversation in its entirety, so as not to fall prey to speculations about what he meant by this or that sentence). This very Cardinal played an important role in my life: even with the perspective of hindsight, I dare to say that it is precisely thanks to him that I remained in the Jesuit order for as long as I did, because I believed that if Carlo Maria Martini was a Jesuit, it meant that they were decent people who had important things to do and say. I dreamt of being one of them. That is why I 'Polonized' approximately ten of his books, because it seemed to me that, if Polish Catholics read them, they would start thinking the way he did. That is why I included a conversation with him in the quarterly that I mentioned before, because I was interested in how he managed as the Cardinal for the largest diocese in the world (almost 10 million faithful). I observed his methods; I was interested in the 'cathedral for non-believers' that he started, in which everyone said what they really thought, rather than what one is supposed to say. He also did not hesitate to happily engage Umberto Eco – who was through with Christianity and Italian Catholicism – in conversation. Even earlier, as the

Rector of the Papal Bible Institute, he established contacts with schools all over the world, encouraging his students to study at the Hebrew University in Jerusalem alongside Israeli students. All of this seemed so obvious to me, so worthy of imitation, of taking on as an approach in Poland as well. I tried, but it did not work.

Martini and I met, along with my wife, in Jerusalem. This was after his lecture at the Hebrew University in 2005, when he received a doctorate *honoris causa*. In the lecture he said much about the Bible as a shared source of faith for Jews and Christians, also evoking his philosophical studies, which he readily forgot when he discovered the world of the Bible. It was this very lecture that became the pretext for another meeting, in the beautiful house of Jesuits in Jerusalem next to the majestic King David Hotel. It was a conversation about philosophy, the Bible, or perhaps it was just about life. Cardinal Carlo Maria Martini wanted to die in Jerusalem. The city had a particular meaning for him. He did not want to tell people what to do, or broadcast the need for dialogue. He wanted just to live there and peacefully study, read and pray.

So now you know, dear Zygmunt, why messianic desires had a human face for me. If there were more such faces, perhaps we would now be having a different conversation about our past experiences; maybe there would be fewer burns and wrongs. I dare to believe that there might even not be any – we would only remember our own insufficiencies, which mobilized us to a more solid acquaintance with the other side. So I imagine to myself – and acknowledge you as correct, without reservations – that man is able, but somehow we don't know so much about this; we don't speak of it often enough. It is not what he is able to do that occupies our attention, but rather his flaws, mistakes and wrongs – the burns it is so hard to forget.

Zygmunt Bauman   Man is indeed capable – but within limits; we are not gods, after all. But within these limits, man not only is capable, but SHOULD be capable, and for proper fulfilment of this obligation man bears responsibility – regardless of whether he prostrates himself before God or denies His existence. But as for the 'life experience, or concrete events, or meetings' that you rightfully invoke – the occurrences which laid open some tracks while barricading some others – these took place in different expanses: on the 'messianic' territory in your case, and on the

'Promethean' one in mine. As the Messiah is the messenger of
God, then no matter what we do, the Second Coming does not
depend on us, and thus in some strange sense we can perceive
waiting for the Messiah as a way of excusing our inactivity, neglect
and blunders, or, what is worse, our consent to the injustices of
the world and our postponement of the need to redress them until
the Second Coming. Prometheus, however, stole the secrets of the
gods and revealed them to humans, leaving thereby no room for
human excuses – but also equipping mankind with the pretext for
clothing themselves in the robes of gods and laying claim to godly
powers and prerogatives. The one 'side-effect' is neither more
appealing nor less dangerous than the other; there is no rose
without a thorn. You were aggrieved by words unmatched by
actions; I was by actions that contradicted words. You followed
Cardinal Martini, for whom the word was just as important as it
was to you, and who did everything he could to make it flesh. In
my life (*ceteris paribus, toutes proportions gardées*...), a similar
role was played by Zdzisław Bibrowski, from whom I learned to
distinguish between healthy social bodies and cancerous growths.
I confided my debt to him in conversations with Roman Kubicki
and Anna Zeidler-Janiszewska.[1]

But I will return briefly to Coetzee, this time to recall his
bemoaning the poisonous effect that faith in the superhuman or
divine provenances of the market has on the human soul and on
human co-existence.[2] God did not create the market, Coetzee says,
nor did the Zeitgeist. And if we, human creatures, 'made' the
market, we can just as well 'unmake' it, or give it a more gentle
and friendly form. It is not necessary for the world to be an
amphitheatre for kill-or-be-killed gladiators; or a racetrack where
the runners only care about forcing their way to the front and not
letting anyone else catch up. It is also not necessary for neighbours
to compete with each other and ruin their cities in the process,
and for national economies to race instead of jogging in each
other's company. None of this is a pre-ordained – and certainly
not a final – choice.

We can still hold out hope that the words will *become* flesh.
But we can also invest our hope in rolling up our sleeves and
transforming the word into flesh. You quote Horace. But I see his
non omnis moriar as a reminder that private life has more-than-
private consequences – and as a warning, that it is not only *not*

worth it, but *impossible*, to live as if it didn't, and one is not permitted to tell oneself that such a way of living can be found. Because I am 'not entirely a corpse', regardless of whether I heeded that reminder or let it fall on deaf ears – or, having heard, ignored it – the traces of my (your, our) commitments and deeds, just like those of my (your, our) indifference and inactions, will be tattooed on the body of the world one way or the other. As, for example, we have recently caused, and are still blithely causing, our descendants to be up to their eyes in debt incurred by us, long before their birth, in the course of our consumerist orgy and lives on credit.

This is what I want to talk to people about, and this is the very thing I want them to listen to. And it is this in which I invest my hope that they might listen. Because it *depends on them and them alone* whether what is humanly possible will get done – or, on the contrary, neglected and overlooked. We will not overcome our human limitations, and God protect us from trying to; let us avoid playing at an omnipotence that we ascribe to God. We are not gods, and that is why not everything is attainable by our merely human strength – but what is within our power will amply suffice for rendering our lives *valuable and worth living* (because devoted to repairing the wrongs of the world – making the world more hospitable to humankind than it heretofore was and continues to be).

Buoyed by these hopes, I put my message into a bottle and entrust it to the waves. I know, only too well, that these hopes may prove in vain; you do not have to convince me of this – I know it from my own experience, and not only from that. José Saramago, another author I deeply respect and love, in a journal entry dated 16 November 2008, bemoaned that 'the handful of sensible things I've said in my life have turned out after all to be of absolutely no consequence'. He wondered: 'Do we talk for the same reason we perspire? Just because we do?' But then he remembered his grandfather Jeronimo, who, 'in his final hours went to bid farewell to the trees he had planted, embracing them and weeping because he knew he wouldn't see them again'. And he added: 'It's a lesson worth learning. So I embrace the words I've written, I wish them long life, and resume my writing where I left off.'[3]

Amen.

SO   On messianic and Promethean temptations, we are in agreement. Both, if one succumbs to them, have negative consequences
for human co-existence. Detaching words from reality is the
scourge of all idealistic or ideological projects. But there is a
crucial – and in the Polish context I would even say fatal – difference. By introducing the figure of Carlo Maria Martini and his
desire to humanize the institution of the Church, I was really
trying to bring the Catholic Church back to Earth. It seemed to
me that Martini was one of a very few representatives of the hierarchy who did not stop being himself, he did not play a role, but
he unceasingly tried to justify rationally his beliefs and life choices.
In brief, he did not surrender his mind entirely, but continuously
demonstrated the possibility of being a thinking person within that
institution. What is more, it seemed to me that the media perceived
this sense of reality of his, and challenged his views with those of
others. Martini emerged unscathed from these confrontations –
he showed that Catholicism with a human face was not a merely
theoretical proposition. His voice played an important role in
anticlerical Italy. You, Zygmunt, by referring to Colonel Zdzisław
Bibrowski and the role he played in your life in the late forties in
the PRL, in a conversation with Anna Zeidler-Janiszewska and
Roman Kubicki, humanized a period often demonized by many
Poles, the so-called 'Stalinist period'. From your descriptions
emerges a person who serves the regime and strives, not only to
preserve his own humanity, but also to protect the humanity of
others. And this seems to me to be a crucial element of our contemporary story. In order to go on weaving it, we need these
concrete faces and their presence in order to understand eras that
have been submitted to overly careless descriptions, and are fading
into black and white. It is precisely people like Martini and
Bibrowski who remind us that it is not ideas but people who create
history. We need them in order to recover the past, or rather to
wrest it from demagogues who either canonize or demonize it,
depending on the expectations or needs of society. In other words,
when I look for traces of hope, what I have in mind is precisely
these kinds of complex tales of human fate.

  I am not sure whether you will agree with me that this kind of
work on the past (because it is work, struggling with recalcitrant
material that is cooling before our very eyes) is absolutely necessary to our lives – as much as air, even – if we don't want to fall

into a vicious cycle of repetition: more specifically, into imprison-
ment in the curse of ideology, which no one will free us from,
unless we do it ourselves. In this sense your sociological sensitivity
has a healing power against the forces of these ideological traps.
It was, after all, the effort to escape from a system imposed in
the name of fidelity to facts that was a source of problems for
you, and, ultimately, of exclusion from the clan of mandarins
obeying the orders of the sovereign. Today's sociologists of religion face similar (though perhaps not as painful) problems when
the results of their studies are displeasing to leaders of religious
institutions.

But you somehow succeeded, you broke through with your own
vision of the world and today you stand among its defenders,
although its official supporters have long since passed into the
dustbin of history. Even today's Left finds its most faithful allies
among erstwhile revisionists. The most orthodox members have
left to serve other masters. In this I perceive the sources of our
hope and optimism and a real chance to extricate ourselves from
the claws of the aforementioned recurrences. What is interesting
is that it is precisely sociologists, and particularly Ulrich Beck,
whom I have mentioned several times, who give a helping hand
to those seekers who are blindly groping for a path. Allow me,
this time, to refer to a somewhat broader claim of his. It is all the
more apropos because, in some sense, it relates to both the fears
of Coetzee and the hopes of Saramago that you mentioned. In his
book, *A God of One's Own: Religion's Capacity for Peace and
Potential for Violence*, Beck claims that 'secular society must
become post-secular, i.e. sceptical and open-minded towards the
choices of religion'.[4] And he adds: 'Permitting religious language
to enter the public sphere should be regarded as enrichment, not
as intrusion. Such a change is no less ambitious than the general
toleration of secular nihilism by the religions.' I not only agree
with the assertions of the author of *World Risk Society*, but also
see in him one escape from rising religious fundamentalism. This
kind of openness could help the faithful stop fearing secularization, and various humanists and rationalists can discern an ally of
post-secularism in religion's return to the public sphere. On the
one hand, Beck writes about religion's meaning in a secular world,
and thus one can see him as a representative of post-secularism;
on the other hand, however, he speaks unequivocally about the

need to change the form of this presence, which in turn connects
him to secularism. The main thesis of *A God of One's Own* goes
something like this: the potential for violence contained in religion
can be neutralized using syncretism and the principles of subjective
polytheism. But the idea here is not so much a return to the many
gods of antiquity as an acceptance of the principles of a 'polymythism' postulated by Odo Marquard, which you, Zygmunt,
referred to at the beginning of our conversation. It is thanks to
you that I read his essay 'In Praise of Polytheism', in which I
encountered this sentence: 'Persons who, in their living and story-
telling, participate, polymythically, in many stories, are free, by
virtue of one story, from the other, and vice versa.'[5] From this new
perspective, the faith of others is no longer perceived as a threat,
but – quite the opposite – as a chance to enrich one's own faith.
Including others in one's own way of experiencing religion, one
not only learns something from them, but also learns more about
oneself. I do not need to emphasize that the kind of understanding
of religion, particularly Christianity, that Beck proposes stands in
decided opposition to traditional ways of understanding religious
realities. It is hard to imagine a greater contrast than the one
between, on the one hand, God and a faith shaped by one's own
choices, and, on the other, the objective and orthodox doctrine of
Christianity, which one is meant to learn and adopt.

It seems that Beck is right when he seeks the origins of the
conception of a 'God of one's own' in the Reformation, particularly in the thought of Martin Luther. Today, in the period of late
modernity, none of the religions, including those with a worldwide
reach, can limit themselves to their own theodicy, but must take
account of other perspectives, and in this sense must become
cosmopolitan religions. If religion understood in this way is not
broadly accepted, then every currently existing form of religiosity
will be threatened by fundamentalism. Is it not a paradox, that
adepts of theological scholarship find comfort in the observations
of a sociologist and sceptical philosopher? Maybe that is why it
is worth sweating it out together and not giving up? It seems to
me that an increased closeness is becoming unavoidable.

ZB '[A] person who serves the regime and strives not only to
preserve his own humanity, but also to protect others'; this is what
you write about Bibrowski, but also about Martini, and yet again

you hit on the crux of the issue. The fact that both 'serve[d] the regime' was, I think, a necessary condition of this preservation of the humanity of 'others', like you or I – faithful to the regime and to their own choices, but aware that there was something in this regime that they were unable to swallow. The instinctive first response of 'others' to such feelings was a sharpened sensitivity to the whispers from beyond the 'regime', whose contents resonated with one's own doubts. If anything, these 'voices from outside' suppressed personal doubts instead of kindling or confirming them in the way their speakers intended. A question echoed in one's mind: Who is speaking through these lips? Probably Satan? The Antichrist? The spokesman of imperialism? The hireling of disinherited factory and land owners? It cannot be that the Antichrist or the lackey of exploiters is right! It is completely inconceivable that I would listen to their poisonous propaganda, would repeat their words and agree with them...Nurturing doubt instead of suppressing it in oneself means, in practice, inviting Satan's advances and turning, willingly or not, into his agent. Persisting in doubt is betrayal.

The thing is, however, that neither Martini in your universe, nor Bibrowski in mine, could be categorized among the followers of the Antichrist – although the 'orthodoxy', mistaking silent obedience for loyalty, were falling over themselves to claim that they were. Martini was not an atheist; Bibrowski was not anti-Communist. Neither the one nor the other was a renegade or a 'foreign mole' in the congregation of the faithful. Bibrowski was not declaiming the 'Voice of America', nor was Martini preaching the 'Voice of the Heretic'. They were believers much like you or I, and probably their faith was even stronger, because it was put to more of a test than ours – and it was *precisely in the name of this faith* that they rebelled against its being abused, soiled, corrupted and perverted. Both the one and the other obeyed the commandment, that *Amicus Plato, sed magis amica veritas*...In their attitudes and transgressions – in their very lives – they personified the fact – the fact most diligently and fiercely concealed or lied about by all regimes – that dissent does not stem from, nor is a mark of, an indifference to the cause, self-absorption, indolence or betrayal.

In *The Art of Life*, I presented the conclusions that I came to when grappling with the problem contained in its title: namely, that there are two factors at work (not always in harmony!) in establishing a person's life trajectory. One is fate (the collective name for everything that happened / happens / will happen to us but is not of our own making, or due to our influence or choice), and the other, character (the collective name for such aspects of our selves as we can and ought to work on – even if they are not entirely obedient to our efforts). *Fate* determines the range of realistic options; but *character* chooses among those options. Now, reading your reflections, I think to myself that the accomplishment of people of Martini's or Bibrowski's kind was not only to add bravery or recklessness to their character, but also to open themselves up to the options that fate had passed over or left in the shadow, even branded with infamy. People of that kind challenge both character and fate.

In a collection of essays written by Hannah Arendt and dedicated to 'people in dark [read: impenetrable, lacking a beacon] times', there is also an essay about Gotthold Ephraim Lessing, one of the pioneers of the German Enlightenment. Arendt commends Lessing not only for being one of the few philosophers of his time to be sceptical about the predictions/projects of 'universalization' – asserting instead that the ways of being human are by nature varied and diverse and will remain such – but also for being one of yet fewer Enlightenment philosophers who genuinely rejoiced in this prospect, for the same reasons that Marquard, two centuries later, praised the condition he branded 'polymythism' – whose attributes you correctly appreciate.

You cite, with an approval that I fully share, Ulrich Beck's suggestion that 'secular society must become post-secular, i.e. sceptical and open-minded towards the choices of religion.' And: 'Permitting religious language to enter the public sphere should be regarded as enrichment, not as intrusion. Such a change is no less ambitious than the general toleration of secular nihilism by the religions.' But there is a hitch, dear Staszek, in that it is far from clear who, in our downright disorganized, polycentric and polyvocal world, is entitled and empowered to grant approval – or, for that matter, to refuse imprimatur. And another snag: what forces and holders of which standpoints will be (with or without permission) eager to engage that 'informal, open cooperation' whose model has been sketched in both Beck's and Sennett's visions? The camps whose opening onto the world (for their own good and for

the good of the world!) you postulate are likely to flee – as the
devil is believed to fly from holy water – from a dishevelled and
disorderly, garrulous and multi-voiced world – refusing to play
the role of just one of many equally entitled to be heard. They are
not likely to surrender their up-front privilege of assuming axiomatically what in a polylogue needs still to be argued and debated
in order to command agreement. Arguments cannot reach plugged
ears; after all, those ears have been plugged in order to prevent
arguments from reaching them, and that is why those who plug
their ears usurp the one God as their exclusive property and leave
no room for *personal* (individually – on one's own responsibility
– construed and acknowledged) Gods. And, as long as ears remain
plugged, letting religion '[enter] the public sphere', the magnani-
mous and solemn declarations voiced by people with eyes and ears
wide open will not amount to much, and will not change much
in the state of the world.

In other words, the crux of the matter is the fulfilment of a still
unfulfilled prayer of the past master of the art of aphorism, Georg
Christoph Lichtenberg, written sometime between 1773 and 1775:
'Teach me to speak to men's hearts without what I say doing what
I did not intend to the fragile system of their convictions [...] and
thy fame shall resound through the millennia.'[6] Lichtenberg, like
myself, does not seem to have expected that this prayer would be
listened to – adding, upon reflection, that if, having taken the love
of truth as his only guide, he 'goes to meet all I regard as error
without exclaiming *I regard that an error*, and even less *That is
error*', he does this thanks to 'philosophical circumspection', a
virtue given to but a few among us.

'The prejudices of the individual, far more than his judgments,
constitute the historical reality of his being'[7] – this is what Hans-
Georg Gadamer opined (pessimistically, or simply soberly?) years
ago, sitting down to write his monumental *Truth and Method*;
in that oeuvre, his *magnum opus*, he claimed that 'interpretive
presuppositions remain at play: reflection cannot overcome them
in the name of the autonomy of reason, certainty, or any other
all-encompassing principle – because a true "engagement with
the Other" cannot take place without "questioning the self"'.[8]
In his view (which I wholeheartedly endorse), there is only one
path to knowledge, to mutual understanding (clearing the site
for argumentation as such, and particularly for the kind of

self-questioning that such clearing would demand): namely, *Horizontverschmelzung* – 'fusion of horizons'. And the fusing of horizons, in my sociological interpretation (in keeping, I think, with Gadamer's philosophical intentions) does not start from the crumbling of presuppositions, but from crushing the barriers between various human habitats (to borrow Bourdieu's term), or – in other words – between material and ideational spheres of human experience.

In its turn, that crushing of barriers is an outcome of interlocking the areas and overlapping the contents of human experience, bringing together what had been previously held separate and denied properly robust contact, or had even furiously objected to facing each other, point blank. This crushing will not happen without an effort to debunk the falsehood, unmask and disavow biases and prejudgments – though, in the final account, the fusion of horizons will not be the doing of philosophers, but of the human mode of being-in-the-world. It is not, it cannot be, a *preliminary condition* (we would have to wait for a long time, in vain, if it were – if we had to wait for it to be met!), but a *product*, of 'informal, open cooperation'. Postponing the exercise of 'fusing horizons' until a time when you have won the battle over the ownership of truth is like putting the cart before the horse. We won't get far that way – though I have to admit that cracking the whip, however futile it may be, can make the waiting time more pleasurable.

SO   Seeking the sources of our hope, we arrived at the inescapable – we are necessary to each other. It is especially thanks to each other that we exist, or rather that we become aware of our personal, ultimately not so contemptible, *conditio humana*. Because, after all, what is the melding or fusion of horizons that you and Gadamer are describing, if not an elementary and honest reckoning with our way of being? Bourdieu's same habituses sleep and so lurk within each of us, waiting to free us from thought and the routines that govern us. I will recall a sentence, whose authorship has been lost in a multiplicity of citations: 'God, grant me the serenity to accept the things I cannot change, the courage to change the things I can, and the wisdom to know the difference.' Whether these are the sighs of a religious soul or of a loyalist from the Chinese court is not important right now. What is essential is

the very need to grasp the limits of possible change and the necessary respect for the current order. This is a different variant of the
dichotomy of fate and character introduced by you in *The Art of
Living*. You say, Zygmunt, that people of Bibrowski's and Martini's ilk are able and willing 'to open themselves up to the options
that fate had passed over or left in the shadow'. This perspective
on the role played by these people very much appeals to me, but
ultimately isn't every meeting like this? We wrest from fate ever
larger swaths of its territory and we are no longer terrified, as the
wise Greeks were, by the inevitability of fate. We take it into our
own hands, even if not everyone likes it. A majority would like to
program us, establish trajectories and force us to change the direction of our lives, to choose a path that it has determined to be
better and more beneficial to us. In the Bible it is stated that you
recognize God only after, never during, and definitely not before.
I would broaden this observation to include meetings between
people. But, as with Biblical meetings between people and God,
so too our meetings with people, or near-misses, are crucial to our
consciousness and readiness for change.

Because, after all, it is not that we *are* – but that we *become*.
We don't know who we are, but we constantly find out from
people close to us, who make us aware of it. Of course I remember
your wise observations on the subject of readiness to accept a
different point of view, or simply a different person. Everyday
observation confirms your scepticism more than it does my optimism. We are confronted with the closing of ranks and increasingly violent, not to say brutal, combat with the enemy – whether
it is an actual enemy or an invented one. To the one being destroyed,
it is irrelevant – actual or invented, sooner or later there will be
the experience of an energetic blow from a sabre or machete.
There is no way around it – that is the limit of my optimism. But
I persist in it, I do not stop believing; even if that limit is the
exhaustion of the one wielding the sword, sooner or later he will
reach it. The examples of the former Yugoslavia or Rwanda
confirm this, though it in no way reduces the tragedy of the
victims.

Allow me to recall a fragment of *Truth and Method*, because
your reference reminded me of my own fascination with Gadamer,
whom I had the occasion to meet during my theological studies
in Naples. My Jesuit lecturers gladly reached for him in order to

make us, the adepts of sacred arts, aware that this German philosopher had more to say about them than St Thomas Aquinas had. Here is the fragment:

> Hence the horizon of the present cannot be formed without the past. There is no more an isolated horizon of the present in itself than there are historical horizons which have to be acquired. *Rather, understanding is always the fusion of these horizons supposedly existing by themselves.* We are familiar with the power of this kind of fusion chiefly from earlier times and their naiveté about themselves and their heritage. In a tradition this process of fusion is continually going on, for there old and new are always combining into something of living value, without either being explicitly foregrounded from the other.[9]

That is what Hans-Georg has to say, and in this assertion of his I also read the story of our meeting, Zygmunt, and of our attempts to investigate why it happened and why we try to explain it to ourselves. I come to the conclusion that it is yet another example of a melding of horizons, which brings a new understanding of what brought us to this point. Simultaneously, I am aware that it is not a melding that eliminates differences or variations, but rather brings them out, and, if I can say so – at least from my point of view – ennobles them. I do not see the fact that, in entering into dialogue and risking an encounter, I always emerge changed as a threat, or as heroism. That is what Walter Ong, with whom I spent the last few years, seemed to suggest. He would often say that true dialogue depends on consent to change, to switch one's own perspective (including a religious one). I acknowledged him as correct and enthusiastically repeated it to others. Today I am inclined to go a step farther and say that, without change (so this is not only about consent or permission, but about a prior decision that it will always be this way) there is neither meeting nor dialogue.

In other words, it seems to me that we have entered into the same kind of self-consciousness: that maintaining the state of 'before' is an act of infidelity and disloyalty towards the encountered Other and ultimately towards one's own self. As the author of long conversations about identity, you know this better than I. I was also made aware of this by the philosopher Leonidas Donskis, who is indebted to you in his writings about identity as something problematic (*Troubled Identity and the Modern World*) which causes difficulties, not only for Lithuanians.

And one more word about what you say: 'They are not likely to surrender their up-front privilege of assuming axiomatically what in a polylogue needs still to be argued and debated in order to command agreement. Arguments cannot reach plugged ears; after all, those ears have been plugged in order to prevent arguments from reaching them.' This is true. But the point is not to forcibly open ears or hearts that have little desire to be opened. Rather, the idea is to reach those who perk their ears up to listen, whose troubled hearts search for solace. Those are the people I have in mind; they are the ones I would like to reach, to meet with and speak to, so we can collectively enjoy a change of fate. Are there too few of them, too few of us? Innovations have never reached many people. They had to be tested in the fires of rejection, mockery and persecution. The first does not surprise me; I have experienced it so often that I finally recognized that it will always be this way; the second does not interest me because it speaks to those jeering rather than the things being taunted. About persecution I will remain silent, because as I surmise, at least in the case of our 'circle of civilization', this has ended. Often, I would like to see pluralistic thought succeed in crumbling, or at least softening, the rocky cliffs of prejudice and preconceived notions. But I am not the first to stumble over these cliffs.

But I am also not the first to see radical change in myself and others. I will refer to only one example, but one that is crucial to our conversations. My perspective and religious experience underwent a deep and radical change under the influence of encounters and conversations with concrete people, whom nobody else before me had met in such a way: that is, with an interest and a desire to understand. Earlier, these had been occasions for conversion, or persuading others of the error of any beliefs different from Catholic ones. This mainly concerns my meetings with atheists and Jews. The first taught me respect for disbelief and the possibility of living with one's deepest convictions, and the second showed me that Judaism is not one of many religions, but an important and vital supplement to Christianity, or maybe the reverse. But that is a topic for a different time. I will only say that, thanks to my Jewish friends, I understood that Christianity, too, is part of the vital extension of faith in the God of Abraham.

If I can describe things somewhat poetically, Father Jan Twardowski once published a volume of poetry with the title, *I Did Not Come to Convert You*. I knew Father Twardowski; I can even say that I was friends with him, or at least he always welcomed me into his green tree hollow by the Church of the Visitation Sisters in Warsaw on Krakowskie Przedmieście. He not only did not want to convert, he was also interested in the world and in people. Probably for this reason, he attracted many people to himself and to God. I am also interested in people and, although I do not attract them to God, I have the impression that my interest in them awakens their faith in themselves, and that is enough for me.

ZB   You ask (yours being, of course, a rhetorical question): 'opening themselves up to the possibilities that fate had passed over or left in shadow [...] ultimately isn't every meeting like this?' Yes, it is, or at least it has the chance to be. Or, in other words: it is, if it is a meeting worthy of the name. Buber distinguished between *Begegnungen* and *Vergegnungen*, recommending the former, and warning against the latter. *Begegnungen* by definition leads not to 'blending' (this eventuality you wisely discard!) but to understanding each side's standpoint, or to such a form of cohabitation as would enrich the life of both sides – broadening the range of possibilities for options heretofore unnoticed, and therefore non-existent (as Ludwig Wittgenstein puts it, to understand is to know how to go on). Something like the encounter that lasted some thirty-three years between Hannah Arendt and her second husband Heinrich Blücher, beautifully described by Pietro Citati:[10] 'She and Blücher were a pair, different, separate, but helping each other, depending on each other, enduring all trials together, their two faces were reflected in one form, they walked the streets in step with each other. When they were together, they created a world in miniature, where they were protected from all misfortune.'[11] Their meeting, as Citati suggests, brought 'companionship, feeling, community, the word' into a world dominated by 'loneliness, quiet and foreignness' (and such, after all, was the world which they met in and subsequently experienced together). But there are also, in many (maybe most?) cases, *Vergegnungen*, or 'quasi-meetings', misbegotten meetings, misfired meetings (I would describe them as encounters of bodies but not spirits, except that in a world of Facebook and Twitter, 'meetings' do without the proximity of bodies): meetings in which one or both sides do not want understanding, but acknowledgment of mutual impermeability; not a 'fusion of horizons' but a confirmation of their irreparable divergence; not the replacement of silence with words and solitude with community, but the opposite – another proof of the weakness of words and the impossibility of community. Today's way of life and cohabitation favours *Vergegnungen* and devalues *Begegnungen*; we sincerely desire the latter, but that which presently passes for common sense cautions us to avoid them, and the weaker-spirited among us are actually forced to avoid them – in both cases in favour of misbegotten encounters. Allow me to repeat here what I wrote recently for the *Tygodnik Powszechny*:

> Our fundamentally individualized consumerist society manufactures not solidarity, but mutual suspicion and competition. The side effect, ubiquitous in this process, is the devaluation of human solidarity: a refusal or negation of its utility in striving for the fulfilment of individual dreams and the success of personal objectives. The devaluation of solidarity is rooted in the atrophy of care for the common good and for the quality of the society in which the individual's life takes place. As Ulrich Beck, one of the most perceptive analysts of contemporary cultural change explains: on every human individual, in their singularity and lonely efforts at self-determination, and not on some well-functioning collective of whatever tier, does the responsibility fall to seek out and find, in their individual way and within boundaries that are determined by individual resources, *individual* solutions to *socially created* problems (a task of effectiveness and absurdity similar to the guidelines issued to families, counselling them to purchase family shelters for a case of nuclear attack).
>
> Unlike societies that are dominated by a *gamekeeper's* attitude (the protection of all God's creations as entrusted to humankind), or the *gardener's* (assuming responsibility for designing and preservation of order), what is stubbornly and insistently called for today derives from the *hunter's* stance: where what matters is the quantity and size of the hunting trophies and the capacity of the hunter's bag. Care for the fauna populating the hunting grounds, and thus also for the success of future hunts, does not enter into the hunter's concerns. In a society of consumers who see the world as made up of potential objects of consumption, the recommended

strategy for life is to carve out a safe and comfortable niche for exclusive private use – inside a public space that is hopelessly and incurably inhospitable to humans, indifferent to human worries and miseries, densely dotted with traps and ambushes. In efforts of this kind, solidarity is not of much help.[12]

In the currently proliferating *Vergegnungen*, it is not the speakers but stereotypes, prejudgments, imputations and slanders that meet, for which those 'conversationalists' merely serve as speaking-tubes. The point is not mutual understanding but having it one's own way while abasing and denigrating the other party. And I am not thinking here of the hopelessly pig-headed margins only, but also of figures habitually appearing on the proscenium of the public stage and setting the tone for interaction, and the institutions seeing to it that the rest of the nation notes that tone, learns it and follows. In the daily *Vergegnungen* of political elites, every one of the invited luminaries enters the television studio with the dots over their i's already firmly in place, and firm determination to keep them unmoved. Guests on the Polish TV show *Prosto w oczy* ('Straight in the Eyes') do what they can to avoid eye contact. What they struggle to avoid by hook or by crook is not only mutual understanding, dear Staszek, but also conversion of partners in 'conversation'. They wish the opposite to happen: to demonstrate that the sinner is beyond redemption, so hardened that conversion is unthinkable, the chance of them coming to their senses having been irretrievably lost, the gates of Hell already slammed shut behind them. The TV guests evade understanding what their neighbours on the right or left or across the table talk about, because understanding is already temptation – horror of horrors – to agree. Because – I will repeat after you the wise words of Walter Ong – dialogue (or a true meeting of souls, not an exchange of insults) is *consent to change*. It is (this time I will refer to Sennett) an acknowledgment of the possibility of being found wrong – and admitting being wrong.

You write: 'the idea is to reach those who prick their ears up to listen, whose troubled hearts search for solace'. Agreed, the trolls on the margins can probably be written off as a loss, but the real nub of the issue is to figure out how the rest of the solace-seekers could be persuaded to 'prick their ears up to listen', and to come to you rather than to someone else – hoping that solace would be found in your conversation. Not everything, but much, depends on you here. As to the slogan, 'I did not come to convert you', in the title of Fr Twardowski's collection of poetry, it reminds me of the case of Amin Maalouf, a great French writer of Lebanese descent. He confesses that what convinced him to open his eyes and ears to the merits of French culture, and led him to fall in love with what he saw, was the respect with which he, a newcomer from a foreign country with the baggage of a different culture, tradition and faith, was greeted in his new fatherland: respect for his alterity, interest in the values he espoused, deference towards his beliefs displayed by people who did not share them. And he admits that if he had met with different treatment, his interest in and love for everything French would never have been ignited. In other words: he was tempted into 'conversion to French culture' by the fact that nobody stepped forward in its name to convert him, there being no hint of forcing him or even of cajoling.

Knowing France somewhat from reading and from autopsy, I believe that Maalouf was lucky. He came across French people cut to your measure, Staszek, and found himself in their environment. And this environment agreed to protect him from those of a different cast by using the arms of mutual understanding and trust. Very few, unfortunately, are as fortunate as Maalouf was.

And because I have already mentioned Citati, whom I am currently reading, I will mention another reflection of his on the factors that led the Galician Joseph Roth, one of the greatest writers of one of the most tragic centuries, to fall in love with his Austro-Hungarian fatherland:

> The huge fatherland included Slovenians, Czechs, Moravians, Slovaks, Italians, Poles, Jews, Russians, caught them in a patient and thick net. Everything in this world was continuously in a state of constant change: familiar and strange, quotidian and remarkable, 'that, which was strange, became familiar, without losing its colours, and the homeland had the pleasing charm of abroad' [...] It was thus a cheerful and bright place, downright innocent [...] If the world was dominated by emphasis, the Monarchy preferred discretion, restrained passions, a calm tone of voice. It was often irresistibly funny, very much like an operetta put on by third-rate

actors. Roth loved it for that reason, because it was funny and not entirely real.[13]

Is there maybe a recipe for a 'cheerful and bright [...] downright innocent' human co-existence lurking in this, in mutual agreement and for mutual benefit – in this precisely: 'discretion, restrained passions, a calm tone of voice'? And thus also a chance that it could 'become familiar, without losing its colours'?

V

Fusion of Horizons

Stanisław Obirek Well then, let us discuss the fusion or melding of horizons. This is not a subject, it is a life programme. All the more interesting that it is you, Zygmunt, who proposes it, you who have written so much about the levelling of difference in our globalizing world. In this process of melding of horizons, which is especially educational for me, people have opposed globalization, the increase in homogenization, and equalization, by vividly countering it with the specificities of their own biographies. Maybe I will give a few examples of this resistance, or of artistic embedding (giving from oneself and simultaneously accepting from others, which gives a new quality, a new alloy, whose component parts are transformed and ennobled). I will start with the afore-mentioned Amin Maalouf. His *In the Name of Identity: Violence and the Need to Belong*[1] made a big impression on me. What a pity that it is not required reading for everyone who is afraid of immigrants. You are right that he was lucky, but through his own openness and self-consciousness about his own difference, he helped others. Allow me to cite a fragment of this book, which particularly effectively expresses this dimension of mutual openness and its benefits:

> My approach constantly calls for reciprocity, and this is out of a
> concern for both fairness and efficiency. It's in this spirit that I

would first say to one party: 'The more you steep yourself in the culture of your host country the more you will be able to steep yourself in your own'; and then, to the other party: 'The more an immigrant feels that his own culture is respected, the more open he will be to the culture of the host country.' I set out the two equations in the same breath because they support one another, inseparable as the two parts of a stepladder.[2]

This stool is rarely stable. Usually it is dominated by awe at the difference of the new place one lives in, and shame about one's own past, or by a compulsive remembering of the grandeur of the old home, which was abandoned with an unconcealed reluctance, and sometimes also a contempt for 'others'. But I still believe that Maalouf is not an exception, that he is slowly becoming a norm, though one unfortunately rarely referred to.

I am all the more glad that you mentioned Pietro Citati, whose books are descriptions of this very co-existence and co-enrichment of difference. But it is not only about the encounter of difference. It is incredible how Citati was able to convey the meeting of Hannah Arendt and Heinrich Blüm, or recreate the poetic wonder that Joseph Roth felt for the cultural mosaic of Galicia, which was not, after all, a paradise for him. I am also enraptured by Pietro Citati. His immense talent manifests itself, I think, particularly in his incisive, almost aphoristic formulations, with which he can express phenomena typically described in weighty volumes. In the book you mentioned, *Israele e l'Islam: le scintille di Dio* ('Israel and Islam: Divine Sparks'), I note such a sentence about Bruno Schulz: 'When he looked at the ground, Schulz discovered that it was illuminated with light; a fiery column, a Deluge, blossoming into flames, as it did before it was torn from the galaxy. All was creativity and fecund; life-giving material reproducing infinitely, that no Giant needed to create.'[3] And he added: 'Like an ancient writer believing that the task of the artist is to recover, with the help of words, the lost unity of the world.'[4] Such writing about others allows us to believe that the world not only can be, but really is, changed by someone's presence. But he is just as masterful when describing the richness of the world of myths, which have not detached themselves from us: they continue to shape our perception of the world. The only person with a similar power to bring the past to life is maybe Robert Calasso, whom I discovered and fell in love with thanks to Ireneusz Kania. It seems to me that the mythic or polyphonic face of religion is still waiting to be discovered, because there is no reason to forget it and cut ourselves off from its life-giving nectar. Maybe we will return to this subject, because it seems particularly important to me as an illustration of the untapped possibilities of religion's creative potential. I mention this because, for a few years, I have been following interfaith dialogues, which seem particularly interesting to me at points when the participants are brave enough to enter into different worlds and are able to perceive in them aspects that are not so much different from, as complementary to, their own traditions. In other words, it is precisely religion that provides us with countless examples of the fusion of horizons.

This time, however, I would like to spend a moment on the essay of yours that so penetratingly analyses the impossibility of *Begegnungen*, about the scattering of solidarity, or so it seems from the brief fragment you cited. Nonetheless, the lesson of the whole forces one to verify the initial, not especially optimistic, impression. As you write:

> The word 'solidarity' seeks a stable embodiment that it could take on, in a wide variety of ways. It searches blindly, and yet no less determinedly. And it will not stop this determined and passionate search until it finds what it seeks. In this search for the body through the word, we, the residents of the twenty-first century, are both the subject and the object of the search, the point of departure and the eventual goal – but also the travellers along that path, and those who create that path with their own footprints. That path will, at the final count, emerge from the traces left by our feet – but it will be hard to mark its place on a map before that work is accomplished.[5]

And I agree with this tracking of the trails of solidarity, and with the above-cited Richard Sennett and his tripartite formulation of a new humanism ('informal, open cooperation'), so empathetically commented on by you, Zygmunt: in essence, it seems to me like a remedy for our ailments. I cannot add much aside from my own modest experience, which confirms this principle in all of its expanse. Maybe I would add one more element, which would make the entirety less wobbly – empathy. I think that it is precisely the principle of spontaneous kindness that leads to our ability to seize opportunities in flight, blowing on the sparks of good to kindle them into flames of transformative gestures. Without empathy, too much remains nascent, and will never really see the light of day. I know that you do not like this – but I trust that you will forgive me – as once more I will refer to your strategy of awakening and pointing to possibilities of understanding and patiently weaving the threads of comprehension. I am thinking of your speech on 29 September 2012 at the Congress of Christian Culture in Lublin, initiated by Archbishop Józef Życiński. You entitled your lecture: 'The Postmodern Image of Man in Society. Where Are the Sources for a Better Future?' I remember how many not especially generous comments about the present condition of modernity were formulated by this hierarch; in some, I heard references to your thinking as well. And this is what I hear – allow me to cite the opening of your speech:

> The Archbishop of the Lublin Diocese, Józef Życiński, was the originator, driving force, and guardian angel of the Congress of Christian Culture. It is thanks to his tireless concern for the audibility of a moral call threatened with being lost in the tawdry clamour of a consumerist bazaar, and for the visibility of a human dignity that risks being drowned in a flood of vulgarities, idiocies, and the obscenity of a commercialized culture, that we have gathered for the second time – and probably not the last one – in this room. Józef Mirosław Życiński is not in this room, but it is filled to the brim with his legacy: that we are meeting in this room so as to reflect, together, on the fate and future of human morality.[6]

Pure empathy; you see him as an ally. I understand that the people to whom you delivered this address received your words with goodwill, maybe even thinking of a shared task – saving the human standards of today's world.

Is this not yet another example of a fruitful and creative fusion of horizons, one that our opponents have not considered? Is it not possibly a mythical example of mutual influence and enrichment? I am interested in what you make of it?

Zygmunt Bauman   Earlier, Staszek, you reminded me that 'In the Bible it is stated that you recognize God only after, never during, and definitely not before.' Kafka paraphrased this oh-so-accurate observation, wryly noting that the Messiah always comes a day after his arrival. Today's academic wisdom – with its cult of statistics and oblique equation of numerical size with the importance and significance of an event – with its proclivity to ignore the minority or write it off into a margin of error, ennobles and promotes even more this age-old human tendency to un-notice the Messiah in time: that is, when he flounders with his good news in his knapsack in our direction through thickets and woods, the muck and the mire, tornados and snowstorms.

Every (statistical) majority, from prehistoric times onwards, started out as a minority! I cannot shake the feeling that philosophy creeps behind human praxis instead of, as it boasts, leading it onto the right track. I will again call on the help of Joseph Roth:

> the people – in agreeable contrast to the politicians – in no way lives off world politics. The people lives off the soil it tills, the trade it conducts, the crafts it has learned [...] After they have read the newspapers, listened to the speeches, elected the representatives, and discussed the news with their friends, the good peasants, craftsmen and traders – and in the cities, the workers – go back to their homes and workshops.[7]

And there, in those 'homes and workshops', is conceived, born or stillborn, matures or dies in its childhood, as the author of *Trans-atlantyk* would sensibly observe, a fusion of horizons – ruled by its own laws and defiantly insensitive to the tumult and furore on the main stage or the commotion on the proscenium. Whether it comes to be or is stopped in its tracks depends on the human conditions. Some conditions are factories of human solidarity and cooperation, others turn out mutual suspicion, hatred, rivalry and competition that are more effective at guarding mutual separation and estrangement than the casuistry of philosophers or demagogues. Our condition today seems to belong to the second category. But all conditions are, in the final account, cumulative and combinatorial products of human choices. And choices are not made on a stage that we are trained and groomed to gape at, but in the wings, so to speak, where the stage lights rarely, if ever, reach. No wonder that, to philosophers and sociologists, and probably to theologians as well (all of them insisting that their own ideas are worthy of recording, whereas those of other scribblers are unworthy of being treated seriously), the Messiah comes a day after his arrival, and maybe even later. And even then, only if during his travels he's managed to avoid being stoned to death on the instigation of false Messiahs.

When you ask, in connection to the events in Lublin, 'Is it possibly a mythical example of mutual influence and enrichment? I am interested: what do you make of it?', how much I would like simply to agree, without hesitation and unreservedly. But common sense, restrained by experience, and time and again held back from exaltation, suggests: well, it is but an *attempt*. Nothing more than an attempt. Maybe an unsuccessful one – one of many such. But I would also add right away: the defeat of trial(s) is not a *proof* that the time has arrived to stop trying. At most, defeat can serve as an *excuse* to stop trying. And a proof and an excuse are not the same thing, though all too often confused! The fusion of horizons is the foundation of a coming together and interweaving of human life practices and experience. Without this coming together and interweaving, urged on by trust, friendship, respect and desire for cooperation, the fusion of horizons has nothing to expect. But all those conditions filter down, each on its own moved by its own momentum – similarly to the Messiah: unperceived, unnoticed and unobserved, by the logic of neighbourhood and daily interactions. What on the level of Huntington's 'clash of civilizations' seems impossible, on the level of neighbourly interaction is practically inexorable necessity. And in that, there is hope.

SO   I really like your revision of the Biblical idea that we find out about what is important after the fact. So, are we left with the unknown and the blind groping in front of us? Because, after all, we are not in a state to inquire whether the direction we have chosen is the one that will allow us to see the approaching Messiah – as you so accurately observe, Zygmunt – 'when he flounders with his good news in his knapsack in our direction through thickets and woods, the muck and the mire, tornados and snowstorms'. But maybe in this, paradoxically, we should seek our rescue? Maybe there is none in this case, as in the most important story of Bruno Schulz, which was allegedly to have the title 'Messiah', which was not preserved. Because each of us must write their Messiah anew, or rather, is already writing it by the mere fact of existing. While we are talking about the Bible, it is worth recalling this meaningful verse from the first book of Genesis, ch. 26: 'Then God said, Let Us make man in Our image, according to Our likeness.' In the next chapter it is slightly different: 'And the Lord God formed man of the dust of the ground, and breathed into his nostrils the breath of life; and man became a living soul.' So we really do not know how it is, whether we are something of the dust of the earth and only fed with the breath of life, or whether we are the image and likeness of God. Maybe this is what causes tensions and the 'clash of civilizations'. Some see the traces of God where others see worthless dust, which muddies their own divinity. Others are burdened by the image of their own mediocrity and, suspecting others of the same, cannot take joy in their existence.

Maybe this is a strange and certainly unorthodox interpretation of a sacred text, but it resonates, I think, with the scepticism of the Galician boy so wonderfully evoked in Joseph Roth's excellent story. It reminded me of my grandfather Franciszek, whom I cannot recall ever seeing with a book or newspaper in his hands, let alone a pen. But he enthralled me with his eloquence and his understanding of the undeniably extremely complicated intricacies of the PRL-era village. His comical monologues, which he recited in my presence, and which other than me only the horses listened to, were actually paraphrases of the speeches of Władysław Gomułka, and they were my real initiation into a world wider than politics. What is interesting, is that Grandfather maintained a far-reaching aloofness in regards to priests and the Church. He simply stayed silent. Interesting that, towards a dangerous – even, in his view, omnipotent – government, a Polish peasant maintained an irreverent distance, but towards a weakened Church he remained silent, only went to church once a week and probably had his own opinions.

I have no idea what came over me and why I am remembering Grandfather Franciszek. Maybe it is through a personal fusion of horizons, which you described so poetically, that I must recall this sentence so as to remember it well and introduce it into practice. You write that the fusion of horizons 'is the foundation of a coming together and interweaving of human life practices and experience. Without this coming together and interweaving, urged on by trust, friendship, respect and desire for cooperation, the fusion of horizons has nothing to expect.' Maybe in this attitude of maintaining a healthy distance from the commotion of the world, so praised by Roth, there is some kind of key to that world's salvation, or at least its transformation? Really, the experience of my childhood can, and perhaps should, be extended to cover that of Polish peasants, also Russian, Lithuanian – maybe even just European – peasants, whose voices were audible only in their huts, and whose wisdom could only be transmitted through direct communication. It did not occur to anyone, certainly not to those very peasants, to write their words down – because God forbid, someone might read and misunderstand them.

As you can easily surmise, Zygmunt, I am echoing here no more or less a figure than Plato himself. Although he wrote so much, and shaped the European (is it only the European?) perspective on the world and the human to such a great degree, he did not completely trust the written word and counselled extreme caution regarding it – particularly when it came to the most important matters. He wrote about this in the *Phaedrus*, expressing his reservations through the voice of Socrates, and then stating them directly in the *Epistles*. These are known issues, but it may be worth recalling them, because they are not obvious to everyone. In the Seventh Letter, written to friends, he says: 'There neither is nor ever will be a treatise of mine on the subject. For it does not admit of exposition like other branches of knowledge; but after much converse about the matter itself and a life lived together, suddenly a light, as it were, is kindled in one soul by a flame that leaps to it from another, and thereafter sustains itself.' You will admit that it is astonishing to consider that this is the writing of one of the greatest philosophers in human history. It is simply impossible to grasp how the 'creator of Platonism' could assert that 'For this reason no man of intelligence will venture to express his philosophical views in language, especially not in language that is unchangeable, which is true of that which is set down in written characters.'[8] This will not give Plato any peace, and he returns to it in the incredible *Phaedrus*. This is sufficiently astonishing for me, still closely tied to my own peasant roots, to again allow myself to quote the Platonic text once more. This time his reservations about writing were expressed particularly clearly. Socrates invokes the words of the Egyptian King Thamus to the inventor of writing, Theuth, which perhaps still hold true for us today:

this discovery of yours will create forgetfulness in the learners' souls, because they will not use their memories; they will trust to the external written characters and not remember of themselves. The specific which you have discovered is an aid not to memory, but to reminiscence, and you give your disciples not truth, but only the semblance of truth; they will be hearers of many things and will have learned nothing; they will appear to be omniscient and will generally know nothing; they will be tiresome company, having the show of wisdom without the reality.[9]

Socrates also formulates the prerequisite of interpreting speech, without which we cannot truly understand it:

You would imagine that they had intelligence, but if you want to know anything and put a question to one of them, the speaker always gives one unvarying answer. And when they have been once written down they are tumbled about anywhere among those who may or may not understand them, and know not to whom they should reply, to whom not: and, if they are maltreated or abused, they have no parent to protect them; and they cannot protect or defend themselves.[10]

Maybe the caution of the peasant is justified, and the things that various 'smart alecs' write about them has little to do with what they really think. These thoughts came to my mind not only because of your interest in Roth's story, *The Bust of the Emperor* ('Die Büste des Kaisers'), but also during recurring discussions on the topic of the legacy of the peasantry in today's Poland. As it seems to me, this subject causes many misunderstandings and unwarranted feelings of superiority.

I do not know whether we will have the occasion to return to this topic, so I will allow myself to recall Wiesław Myśliwski's interesting – or so they seem to me – observations on the subject of the end of peasant culture, which after all was never fully known, nor fully valued, particularly by the Polish intelligentsia, who 'aside from some exceptions, did not know very much about peasant culture and did not want to know'.[11] And this is a pity, because this decline does great harm to our understanding of who we really are. I am inclined to accede to Myśliwski when he perceives, in the stubborn persistence of the Polish peasantry, the source of the persistence of the identity of the entire society:

'However, in my opinion – tangentially – it is in large part thanks to the peasants that Poland survived. Thanks to their attachment to the land, the language, to faith. The survival of the peasantry was assessed on these three foundations, here and always, from fathers and grandfathers and onwards, regardless of whether Poland was the mother or the step mother, or whether it was at all. And independently of what one knew about it and how one felt about it.'[12] Even if this statement is not short of idealization and nostalgia for the past, it is nonetheless impossible not to see an essential supplement to the discussions of historical politics, or politics in general, that are happening today. If Myśliwski is right, then the most important and most stable way of shaping consciousness is by nonverbal means. There is yet another element of peasant culture tied to this: experience. Myśliwski intentionally does not flesh out what kinds of experiences he means here. They could be perceived as interchangeable with life itself, or with things that simply happen. Myśliwski writes:

> Experience was the foundation of this culture, a vertical – if it can be described this way – experience, meaning generations, and horizontal, meaning communities, in which a person lived. It was above all the experience of the harshness of existence and in this regard we can speak, without exaggeration, about an existential fullness. This experience was not lacking in anything that people as individuals or as a collective could encounter in this world. From this experience emerged the entire philosophical system of this culture, which percolated through human behaviour – such as lullabies – practical or useful wisdom, but also a wisdom of generalizations, assessments and judgments. It basically created a guide with resources for every need, but also a collection of rules, which a person ought to live by. This wisdom manifests itself in humour and irony, saturating peasant forms of joy and celebration, wedding ceremonies, peasant erotics, folk songs, flirtations, etc.[13]

So, we see an oral culture, not bothering to write down what is essential. It was an experience encompassing the entirety of life and preserving community. It expressed that community's identity and difference from others. That shared fate is what made one a peasant. Maybe this is exactly what Joseph Roth has in mind?

Now things are different. If peasant culture has run itself out, what has taken its place? Who really are Poles today? Who am I, ultimately, if I nostalgically remember my grandfather Franciszek and simultaneously find myself completely outside of his world? Once it seemed to me that I was mainly shaped by the world of books, because they granted me entrance into rooms, first in the Church, and later, or maybe at the same time, academic ones. Now these rooms seem to me like an alternative linked to the loss of the world of my childhood. And I am thinking about ways to return to it, though of course I realize that there are no such returns.

I went on a bit too much, perhaps, about my own peasant genealogy, but because I have begun, let me dot the i. I feel myself to be the heir to this silent legacy, and it seems to me that I understand the scepticism towards the world of newspapers felt by the hero of *The Bust of the Emperor*. I not only understand it, I also share it, because it seems to me that today's newspapers, multiplied by various 'Facebooks', 'Twitters' and God knows what other variants of the ever-present internet, seemingly supposed to make our lives easier, actually complicate it and wrap it in a nifty net, creating more and more loneliness. But this, Zygmunt, is a path you have already trod and one that I do not dare to start down without getting altogether lost; I prefer to stay on my peasant's patch. How can we talk about a fusion of horizons here when the entirety of this experience is limited to one, or at most two, generations, and essentially consists of the reproduction of existing forms of behaviour? In spite of everything, I am ready to perceive, in this message of peasant experience, an individual comment on the previously mentioned image of creation in Genesis: I am created by a second me, and in this I locate a source of goodness and uniqueness – without the mediation of a text.

ZB You write, citing Plato that: '"There neither is nor ever will be a treatise of mine on the subject. For it does not admit of exposition like other branches of knowledge; but after much converse about the matter itself and a life lived together, suddenly a light, as it were, is kindled in one soul by a flame that leaps to it from another, and thereafter sustains itself." You will admit that it is astonishing to consider that this is the writing of one of the greatest philosophers in human history.' But I will not admit it. Not without cause was Plato acclaimed as 'one of the greatest philosophers in human history'. Still today, many people – again not without reason – repeat after Alfred North Whitehead that all of Western philosophy is a series of footnotes to Plato.

But to return to the issue of your key inquiry: however few hairs are left on my head, they are all standing on end at the thought of what Socrates would say to Thamus if their conversation were happening in the age of servers and 'cloud computing' (and were Socrates at all conceivable in such an era, which is rather doubtful). Servers have, among other features, a way of stripping us of the things we used to call, with a mixture of adoration and fear, 'tradition', 'legacy' or 'kerugma'. And then (that is, now) tradition shares its fate with the face which the hero of one of Leszek Kołakowski's fairytales left in a pawnshop, counting on it to be safely preserved there until the time he would need it again – not knowing that some urchins had made a ball out of it, and were using it to play soccer in the neighbourhood courtyards.

Warehouses for storing thoughts, and among them the art of writing, were rather late discoveries in human history. Before their invention, oral/audial conversation was the only way to exchange and share ideas, and thus to convey and share knowledge: to teach and learn. 'Wise conversation' – so acutely reconstructed in Thomas Mann's *Joseph and his Brothers* – was for the vast majority of human history the only forge in which deeds and events were recast as history: a meeting point where the diachronic ('vertical') and synchronic ('horizontal') dimensions of human time were consequently intertwined – or in other words, the dimensions of *heritage* and *community*. All of this happened, so to speak, unawares, on its own and from itself, without the help of scholarly writings that dictated the procedures believed to guarantee results, and without overseers or guards. And under those conditions (which ended forever with the invention of writing and the archive), inquiries such as 'Who am I?' or 'What is my place?' would have been objectless or even incomprehensible. Bah, just expressing admiration for the charms of community or tradition, let alone dreaming of their acquisition, composition or rebirth, signals that the legacy is crumbling, having legs too wobbly to stand on. The 'politics' of memory, assuming that the past is a collection of records meant to be arranged and rearranged on archive shelves, sounds the death knell to community and tradition. Such an idea is drawn from funeral banquets.

But it is high time to stop, I have ventured too far. As is clear from the teachings and lessons of Victor Turner, one of the greatest minds in anthropology, it is still far too early to write the obituaries of 'wise conversation' (if the time to do so will ever come). Against the claims of Ferdinand Tönnies, who half a century before presented *Gemeinschaft* ['community'] and *Gesellschaft* ['society'] as two successive but mutually exclusive phases of history, *communitas* and *societas* (as Turner called them, in order to avoid unnecessary confusion over terminology) not only co-exist in every human aggregate, but also each depend upon, and demand, the existence of the other. Without both co-present, our human existence would be inconceivable. And immersion in both at the same time is what we are all sentenced to for centuries to come. They are the warp and weft of the fabric we call human existence. Two strands may compete to be the brightest colour or the broadest stripe, but they are doomed to lifelong collaboration. In other words: for both 'written' (or, now, virtual) and oral culture, one cannot get by without the other. Both exist only in each other's company. There is no returning to a pre-writing or pre-servers era, but, at the same time, some incarnation of 'peasant culture', whose prototype was discovered and recorded by the nineteenth-century folklorists and ethnographers, is still in and with us.

What has changed in the last decade, as Jean-François Lyotard suggested, is the decline of 'grand narratives', but also an attendant crowding of narrations – the density of the crowd and tactile closeness of narration render continuous communication a foregone conclusion. If 'historical politics' did not arise on its own in such conditions, then it would be necessary, as Voltaire would say, to invent it. In our present circumstances, it is not so much the conflict between *communitas* and *societas* that interferes with the clarity and 'self-evidence' of the setting – the domestication and intelligibility of the world – as it is the cacophony of discordant voices and variety of incompatible alterities co-existing in a friction- and conflict-ridden, yet close and intimate, adjacency.

To return to the main topic of our deliberations, or to translate the currently debated matters into its idiom: it is not so much about the battle between monotheism and polytheism, as about the stubborn way in which a multiplicity of gods evades synthesis in the context of polytheistic *life*: each of the lives lived in a world of servers, diasporas, information superhighways. How could human orientation in the world not be muddled, when competing politicians pose as historians rewriting history and reselecting the contents of heritage – and, expecting lavish political gains from such exercises, hurry to their prospective electors (and hopefully subjects) with radically simplified (and mutually contradictory) formulas, promising to bring succour to the lost and clarity to the perplexed. Do not be surprised then, that – as you say – you not only understand but share the 'scepticism towards the world of newspapers' felt by the hero of *The Bust of the Emperor*. You are correctly identifying the sources of this scepticism when you observe that 'today's newspapers, multiplied by various "Facebooks", "Twitters" and God knows what other variants of the ever-present internet, seemingly supposed to make our lives easier, actually complicate it and wrap it in a nifty net, creating more and more loneliness'. Isolation in a crowd of solitary people – who, let us remember, remain, willingly or not, in constant touch. If something truly disappeared in the course of my life (and probably also in yours, though it has been to date much shorter than mine), it is the situation in which, as you write, the 'voices were audible only in their huts, and [...] wisdom could only be transmitted through direct communication'. Today your grandfather Franciszek would probably get himself a laptop, and, were he unable to set up a Facebook account himself, he might ask his grandson for help. He would then contribute, like the rest of us, to the 'noise on the line', which many of us vainly struggle to be rid of, and whose mitigation we all desire to one degree or another.

Speaking parenthetically, I envy you your grandfather Franciszek. Mine, Izak, gave up on reciting histories to me after a few failed attempts, probably deciding that I was of a different tribe, and not a worthy partner suitable for 'wise conversation'.

VI

The Disinherited; or, Creating Tradition Anew

Stanisław Obirek   Given that, as you say dear Zygmunt, servers are stripping us of our tradition and inheritance, what is left for us? 'Wise conversation', which you mentioned, following Thomas Mann, and which various forms of writing have irremediably destroyed, is now inaccessible to us. While I agree with you that it is too early to write the obituaries of those conversations, it does seem worthwhile to remember just how much writing reshaped (in ways agreeable to people of the time) our perceptions of ourselves and the world. I cannot resist mentioning two of the great teachers who made me aware of the consequences of the introduction of writing. One is the unequalled and still-writing Jack Goody, and the other, though less prolific, causes a stir with each new book – Jan Assmann. I will mention only one book of Goody's, *The Logic of Writing and the Organization of Society*, which merits careful attention, as it seems to me,[1] though the others are also worth reflecting on. In his opinion it is writing that opened up practically boundless possibilities to rulers, placing power, not only over space, but also time, in their hands. This ability to make use of writing gave them the ability to establish contact with neighbours, and frequently to conquer them. The growing feeling of independence and distance between specific nations, particularly when accompanied by the worship of God, became a spark of conflicts and wars:

With the advent of world religions (and written ideologies), inter-group conflicts were affected in quite another way, both inside and outside political units. Internally one consequences of the increased autonomy of Church and state, of the boundary-maintaining quality of written religion, is not simply the tension, the struggle, between two 'great organizations', but the conflicts between the adherents of different 'world' religions, culminating in wars of religion.[2]

Without writing it might have been similar, but certainly writing simplified and sanctioned these practices of conquest and depend-ence. On the other hand, writing has a double-edged character, and can turn against its employer: 'When you have boundaries, markers of the kind involved in religions of the Book, then you get not only break-away sects but break-away individuals, indi-viduals who are apostates or converts. Conversion is a function of the boundaries the written word creates, or rather defines.'[3] So maybe it is not such a bad thing; what matters is the way it is used. I'd like to consider one more thought from this book, this time directly connected to our subject – namely, religion.

The word heard from God and passed on from mouth to mouth underwent modifications and was adapted to changed circum-stances with relative ease (this is what Goody refers to as its 'incorporating character'). Once written, it became the final and unchanging point of reference:

> In the literate churches, the dogma and services are rigid (that is, dogmatic, ritualistic, orthodox) by comparison; the creed is recited word for word, the Tables of the Lord learnt by heart, the ritual repeated in a verbatim fashion. If change takes place, it often takes the form of a break-away movement (the term 'break away' is used for sects that separate from the mother church); the process is deliberately reformist, even revolutionary, rather than the process of incorporation that tends to mark the oral situation.[4]

What is more, it is precisely religions based on the Holy Book that did not tolerate other competing claims, becoming the one source of Truth. And it is exactly this legacy of writing that bothers me, and which Jan Assmann directs our attention to, so I will cite my own discomforts as partial justification of his claims. Although Assmann's book introduces much clarity into the muddle of human history, there is nonetheless no way to include it among, as you call them Zygmunt, 'politicians [posing] as historians, offering a radically simplified vision, and meanwhile eager for lavish gains, coming to the aid of the lost and perplexed'. Instead, Assmann stirs up and unsettles our comfortable assumptions; at least this is what happened to me when reading the only book of his that is available in Polish, which is devoted to cultural memory. Of the many subjects discussed in *Cultural Memory and Early Civilization*, it is worth mentioning the topic of the creation of a canon of texts that are seen as sacred and that support given regions of civilization. Contrary to what we often think, their beginnings were shocking. Thus, the Jews owe the main framework of their faith to . . . the Persians. It was precisely imperial politics that counteracted the development of local traditions. Of course, the point was not to introduce those beliefs to conquered peoples as foreign elements, but quite the opposite: thanks to the decisions of Persians, Egypt and other conquered peoples discovered their own cultural identity. That is what led to the emergence of the most important book of the Hebrew Torah – the Book of Deuteronomy, whose primary intuition became a paradigm for many later religious traditions. The price of these modifications was high: 'The process of depoliticizing public life began to take effect generally during the Persian period. In Egypt and Babylon was seen the clericalization of culture, during which time the role of representing culture shifted from scribe-officials to scribe-priests; in Israel the transition was from prophets to scholars.'[5]

The clericalization of religion led to its sacralization and stagnation. So it was in Egypt, when memory passed into the control of priests, and so it is in every culture that surrenders the critical ingredient that underpins its prophetic and hermeneutic dimension. Prophets, in questioning the abuse of political power, restore it to its rightful proportions, and 'the learned in writing', thanks to various hermeneutic strategies, allow holy texts to become integrated into changing cultural contexts. In brief, in place of a ritualized liturgy, we find a more flexible hermeneutics. This happened largely thanks to changes in the technology of passing on traditions. Writing's entry into the place of oral tradition made possible a break with a stagnation of ritual: 'It is through the written element of traditions that the dominance of repetition gradually gives way to that of re-presentation – ritual gives way to textual coherence. A new connective structure emerges out of this, which consists not of imitation and preservation but of interpretation and memory.'[6]

These are only a few of the provocative thoughts of Jan Assmann, which I trust are also not without meaning for our contemplation of religion and its presence in our culture. Though I find much benefit in reading both Goody and Assmann, I must also admit that their diagnoses do not depress me, nor do they deter me from reading or writing – quite the opposite. Reconstructing both the 'logic of writing' and 'cultural memory' encourages me to create my own written works, and to calmly reflect on my own memory, both cultural and religious – and on memory without qualification. Both the one and the other surface in gentle conflicts, and sometimes in peasant banter. Because, after all, the point of departure is important and well known, though it always evades arrival and remains concealed. Does this mean the creation of something new, or going around in endless circles?

I am curious what our grandfathers, Izak and Franciszek, would say about this. Because after all, they came from different memories and cultures. Did they realize that they were the inheritors of 'grand narratives' whose loss was mourned by Lyotard, or were they perhaps contented with the small stories of generations of Baumans and Obireks? Did the fact that they were spared the mixing of cultural codes that is the bane of our present day deprive them of the awareness that worlds existing alongside each other did not exist separately, but somehow together? Given that we increasingly suffer from a loneliness and estrangement that are the result of the growing white noise of information, as you were kind enough to agree with me, does this mean that our grandfathers were more strongly and firmly rooted in their communities? Because we are well aware that the storms of history did not spare either of them; rather, it swept away the world they knew before their very eyes. We both observed them; we tried to ask them questions. It is really only today that I realize how many questions I want to ask; at the time, I was only capable of listening to my grandfather's monologues, not understanding much of them. Thus, I am unsure whether we are forging a new tradition or merely translating it, as you aptly put it in the title of a book very dear to me, one that I never stop recommending to my students as compulsory reading.[7]

Zygmunt Bauman I will show my hand: in debates about the relationship between the oral and the written word, my sympathies are with the views of Jacques Derrida, who, as you know, located the roots and productive energies of language in writing, not speech. You yourself, reminding writing (and rightfully so) of its many sins, observe that without it things 'might have been similar, but certainly writing simplified and sanctioned these practices of conquest and dependence'. The written record certainly created the possibility of orthodoxy (and therefore something to be defended from competing views) – but it also brought to life heresy and incentives for schism, and, more generally, for what we call 'critical thought'. This also pertains to its influence on the intricacies of the history of religions: the written record took the key to heaven's gates out of the hands of the elders and gave it to those who knew the arts of reading and writing. It was, in other words, a revolution of hierarchy. It made Luther possible.

Born forty years after Johannes Gutenberg's invention, Martin Luther could demand that the Holy Texts be given back to each and every member of the Church, thus entrusting each of the faithful with the virtue/privilege invested in the message of those texts: the right/responsibility previously reserved for the elders (firstly elders in age, later in rank). Were he born forty years before Gutenberg's invention rather than after, Luther probably would not have hit upon this idea. Though, on the other hand, after Gutenberg's invention, that idea, regardless of whose mind it originated in, was probably preordained. The intolerance of Churches of the Book to which you are opposed was not the fault of writing, but of the Churches' self-defence against the possible 'amateur philosophizing' of your grandfather Franciszek's sort. As you yourself mentioned, in the case of your grandfather, a wise man with a critical mind, that self-defence was quite effective! I doubt that Franciszek read deeply in the Bible. As for the messages contained in Holy Texts, he listened to them in Latin, hearing them in a language he could understand from the lips of a priest on the pulpit. I guess that the story about 'the Cheese and the Worms',[8] which Carlo Ginzburg wrested from the secret archives of the Inquisition, makes visible the fate that would have awaited Grandfather Franciszek if he had tried his hand at authoring religious texts in the way that Domenico Scandella, known in his neighbourhood as Menocchio, bravely but somewhat recklessly did during the period of the Inquisition. I think that we are to a large degree in agreement as to our assessments of the utility of writing, given that you indicate that – despite their apocalyptic suggestions – 'their [Goody's and Assmann's) diagnoses do not depress me, nor do they deter me from reading or writing – quite the opposite.' Indeed.

And now, as to your question, so important for understanding the philosophical problems confronting us – indeed, what would my Izak and your Franciszek say about them? I will point out that a conversation between them probably would not get to the point of debating religious truths, because they were spared, as you say, 'the mixing of cultural codes that is the bane of our present day, [depriving] them of the awareness that worlds existing alongside each other did not exist separately, but somehow together'. This is the crux of the matter! Not in 'grand narratives', but in their pretensions to singularity made visible and real by social practices of separation and exclusion.

Antagonisms could survive the disappearance of the conditions that created them, but for how long, neither you nor I know, and we can't guess. George Steiner once explained Voltaire's, or Holbach's, self-confident certainty as the privilege of their ignorance, of which later history deprived us. Franciszek and Izak owed the solidity of their faith, and humility towards its clerical interpretations (the only such messages that reached them), to a similar privilege. We, however, are handicapped by the knowledge that they lacked.

This is how Ulrich Beck, in his most recent work,[9] explains the contours of knowledge deriving from the daily experience of our contemporaries:

> Different religions are coming into more direct contact. Muslim, Jews and Christians are praying in the same places. With the many millions of believers scattered throughout foreign lands, their one true gods also spread across the globe. They, the lords of the world who brook no rivals, must now learn to live with one another in a confined space. The explosive force of this simultaneity of geographical proximity and social distance is only now becoming tangible when all of their attempts to isolate themselves from each other are already futile [...] What we are experiencing here is the intermeshing and antagonism of the world religions... The one and

exclusive God of the religious other is no longer elsewhere but is here alongside us, in our midst.

In brief: competing monotheisms have no choice but to reconcile themselves to the incurable polytheism of a world that they unavoidably share – and to glean from it the obvious conclusions.

Here lies the problem, though: what conclusions? Are we closer to understanding them than Franciszek or Izak were? Beck cautions: 'The cosmopolitanization of life conditions and experiences of the world does not necessarily generate a cosmopolitan consciousness and mentality. Shocks do not always open people's eyes to the openness of the world.'[10] Coming eye to eye with the universalistic claims of different groups gives rise to conflicts and can lead to violence. At every crossroads, signposts show more than one direction.

SO The adventures of the hero in the book by Carlo Ginzburg that you mention, Zygmunt, were not unique, nor was the way that the Catholic Church dealt with heretical tendencies. One hundred years after Dominico Scandelli, Giordano Bruno was consigned to the flames, to the delight of the masses gathered at the Campo di Fiori. To my knowledge, Ginzburg's insistence that the Vatican Archives be opened constantly encounters bureaucratic obstacles, which is why our knowledge of the Inquisition's practices of control remains incomplete. Stopping the mouths of those proclaiming unpopular views, or burning them at the stake, is of course only one way of controlling the minds of the conquered (indeed, similar things were done by other twentieth-century churches, as well as by totalitarian or authoritarian regimes). Stephen Greenblatt recently pointed out another way, masterfully reconstructing the remembering and forgetting of Lucretius' poem *De rerum natura*, particularly the contributions of the main protagonist of this episode of history, Poggio Bracciolini.[11] These are very informative events and they in many ways illustrate the wisdom of the conviction shared by you and Derrida, that writing contains 'the roots and productive energies of language'. But this raises the question as to whether it is able to serve this function without speech/conversation? If Poggio's Florentine mentors had not infected him with a mania for reading and seeking out the manuscripts of ancient authors languishing in monastic scriptoria, then most likely this work of Lucretius' would never have seen the light of day, and would not have played a role in the changing perspectives of our ancestors. And to complete the picture, I should add that this humanist lover of Greek and Roman antiquities was the secretary for as many as eight Popes, and this was at a not especially prosperous moment for the Papacy. We must also supplement the image emerging from Greenblatt's book with Jean Leclerq's fascinating study of the love of literature that existed alongside the worship of God in Benedictine monasteries for centuries. Without them, *De rerum natura* and other 'pagan' treasures would never have reached us.[12]

I discussed these dilemmas of 'written' and 'oral' with Shoshana, whose opinions I very much value. Shoshana asked me a question that was straightforward but very much to the point: why do you create an alternative – either writing, or speech? Both the one and the other are important to us, and if we are to wrack our brains over something, then it should be over how both are used. She mentioned Adolf Hitler's *Mein Kampf*. Neither the title nor the author's name can be uttered without a shudder of horror and an awareness of its destructive force, both for its readers and for those who found themselves in the reach of their activities. The destructive dimension of the pages blackened by Hitler became clear not at the moment of writing or publication, but when their author began proclaiming his beliefs and way of seeing the world, when it was multiplied by the number of people with radio receivers in Nazi Germany and the countries it conquered. Thus this hideous text was brought to life by speech and the 'democratically' chosen structures supporting it. So there is something to argue about, and it is worth clarifying what we mean when we discuss writing and speech.

I was very taken by the latest reflections from Ulrich Beck – who, as you know, is quite close to me – that you brought up, on the new situation that the world's monotheisms have found themselves in. There is no way to disagree with his conclusion, that 'competing monotheisms have no choice but to reconcile themselves to the incurable polytheism of a world that they unavoidably share'. But there is no sign of this reconciliation; quite the opposite – if anything it is rather the clanging of weaponry (thankfully largely of the ideological kind) that is heard in all directions, and thus far there are no signs of, or resources for, them being silenced. Thus I agree with Beck's warning, and repeat with you: 'The cosmopolitanization of life conditions and experiences of the world does not necessarily generate a cosmopolitan consciousness and mentality. Shocks do not always open people's eyes to the openness of the world.' Maybe I would even sharpen his careful formulation and add that they never open it. On the contrary, they add fuel for chauvinists and fundamentalist demagogues. And the violence that you mention is not a possibility but a fact, one observable even on the streets of Warsaw. Are they not reversible? I do not know, and do not want to assume the form of fortune-teller. I perceive reflexes of self-preservation – unfortunately, not in institutionalized religion. Often that movement fills me with trepidation and arouses naked fear.

Shoshana, when I share these fears with her, always asks: if you perceive the seeds of evil in religion, and certainly do not expect it to come to the rescue, then what do you even believe in? To her, matters are clear. She is blessed with the gift of not believing and is at least not burdened with illusions. But me? When she asks me this, I shyly try to answer that I believe in a Providence that allowed me to meet her, and that I believe that this kind of being together, and faith in the possibility of living in this world, is a form of grace that we have both received. So maybe we have not been completely thrown from the saddle; we not only inherited the world, but we also possess it somehow and can change it within the limits of our powers. And if we cannot change it, then at least we can strive for it to continue being, at least somewhat, our, human world.

ZB You have laid all this out so beautifully, Staszek – and lived through it and felt it, even more commendably; and I think it is precisely in this – in the evidence that one can, as you did, experience life and the world, and, like you, make sense of one's own experiences and share them with others – lies the hope of our and the world's salvation. Though it is also a forceful argument against your sharpening of Beck's thesis in your suggestion that the tremors shaking us *never* open our eyes to the openness of the world. They open our eyes, and widely, even if, by the same token, they tempt us to shut them. After all, he or she who shuts their eyes, won't have to look at his or her own responsibility for the shape of the world, and for the well-being of people in it, in its face. That's a weight off their backs, and one less woe to worry about.

You are right (and deserve credit) when observing that, one way or the other, we somehow possess this world, and, from time to time, here and there, are even able to change at least a small part of it for the better. Given that this world of ours is still in-the-making, the act of its creation yet incomplete, and the work of continuing the creation and its completion has (to recall our earlier conversations) fallen to us, then it is right for us – as for any responsible host – to care for its well-being and attend to its goodness and beauty. I will repeat again Camus' credo: there is beauty, and there are the humiliated. God grant that I never be unfaithful to the one or the other.[13]

John Paul II, when already ill and approaching death, never stopped proclaiming to our world, devoured as it is by greed and resentment, hatred and insensitivity, that 'God is love.' You and I and many of our compatriots would gladly accept such a God; such a God we would find difficult – nay, impossible – to renounce, unless it was along with our humanity.

SO I must confess, Zygmunt, that this credo of Camus' that you mention moved me greatly, so I will repeat it once more, so as to savour it: 'there is beauty and there are the humiliated. God grant that I never be unfaithful to the one or the other.' It resonates all the more in the context of what I have been reading over the past few days – which, I must admit, I could not put down until I had finished it. It was your most recent book, *This is Not a Diary*. The first entry, from 3 September 2010, is already quite moving. It is about your loneliness after Janina's passing, and your efforts to conquer this painful state of solitude. I trust that you will not take it badly if I recall certain, to me very crucial, fragments of your writing. For me they were like an extension, or rather a broadening, of our mutual reflections on the *conditio humana*. Of course, the context of your reflections is also important, and a secondary argument that emboldens me somewhat to chime in with your 'not-diary' is my own fleeting and fragmentary acquaintance with Janina – one deepened, however, by reading her books, which I know were also important to you, particularly in the creation of *Modernity and the Holocaust*. So I will bring up this first fragment:

While adoring solitude, I abhor loneliness. After Janina's departure I've reached the darkest bottom of loneliness (if there is a bottom to loneliness), where its bitter and most pungent sediments and its most toxic effluvia gather. Since Janina's face is the first image I see when switching on my desktop, the rest that follows the opening of Microsoft Word is nothing if not a dialogue. And dialogue means an impossibility of loneliness.[14]

Thus, you give a new definition of dialogue – as a way of conquering loneliness. I like it very much, and perhaps it contains all the others within itself.

I was also drawn to your analysis of secularization as yet another embodiment of a struggle for power, in which there are really no winners, only losers. The fight itself is absurd, because it misses the essence of things, which depends, I believe, on a readiness to acknowledge one's own helplessness in the face of the astonishing plenitude of reality. Neither a declared religiosity treated as a weapon against 'godlessness', nor an unpardonable fight with it, deserves notice, because the mechanisms activated by them are simply hostile to humanity and lead to the enslavement of another person. This way of framing the issue is so different from dominant perspectives in the sociology of religion that I will again allow myself the pleasure of citation, just to enjoy its skilful formulation: 'The true substance of the modern campaign of "secularization" was a power struggle; and the object of that struggle, its stake and its yearned-for prize, was the right to select from the array of competing legitimizing formulae one procedure entitled to claim truth-value for its results, by the same token disqualifying the claims of all other competitors.'[15] You mention, in this context, the unjustly forgotten Ludwig Fleck. Though Thomas Kuhn himself acknowledges a debt to this Polish thinker, even in Poland we talk of paradigm shifts 'as discussed by Kuhn'. Wrongly. Fleck spoke of them earlier and formulated his opinions on the rise of intellectual ideas with more precision. Zygmunt, you supplement Fleck's ideas with an important point pertaining to the (apparent) conflict between science and faith, reminding us that both offer truths to be taken on faith. I suspect that there can never be enough reminders of that, if only to dull knives unnecessarily sharpened for so-called 'enemies' and imagined opponents. How wisely, then, you say, ending your notes devoted to 'dilemmas of faith', under the date of 17 October 2010:

Science's a priori intolerance for all and any alternative entitlement
to be the one speaking-with-authority is a secular extension of
monotheism; a monotheism without God. Both inspired and moved
by the spirit of Jerusalem, the two contenders agree on the indisput-
able need to tame, curb, check, and suppress the cheerful and
carefree wantonness of Athens that left truth to the vagaries of the
agora.[16]

Will this cessation happen? It is hard to predict, but it seems
that all of the consequences of a calamitous rivalry create an effective incentive – at least for the thinkers on either side of the
barricade.

You trace your thoughts, Zygmunt, along the shadows of Janina's passing. But reading the one-year-anniversary entry of 29
December 2010, I would like to write that they are the traces of
the presence of her light. First you recall the words of Eleanor
Roosevelt, 'No one can make you feel inferior without your
consent', and immediately add 'I felt as if I were reading words
spoken about Janina, and by her; words spoken to describe the
logic of her life and to convey the essence of her faith, her own
way of being-in-the-world.'[17] Maybe it is a miracle, which you
write about elsewhere – a miracle happening in a place where we
are capable of observing it, or maybe happening at a time when
we are ready to accept it. In any case, the kind of presence you
describe makes it possible for us to continue living among those
who are gone. They are not gone for good. They simply are. They
allow us to look at the world through their eyes, and in this way
they make change possible. In brief, they make it less threatening,
and certainly less empty.

It seems especially important to me that your 'not-diary' does
not spare the reader warnings, entries evoking concern and fear
for the future (particularly in fragments in which you pause to
sketch the silhouettes of political leaders or economic gurus).
When we look at them along with our departed – to echo the title
of Maria Janion's fantastic book *Do Europy – tak, ale razem z
naszymi umarłymi* ('To Europe Yes, But With Our Dead') – they
are less threatening; they become as if domesticated, native – ours.
I cannot deny myself the pleasure of recalling one more definition,
which you mention almost as an aside, unwillingly. It just so
happens that I am currently giving lectures on globalization and

regionalization, in which I try to define these two tendencies that worry us on a daily basis. In doing so, I naturally use your metaphors, Zygmunt, which have settled comfortably into the Polish language. Like the global green pastures being devoured by international corporations, we see everywhere tourists welcomed with open arms, and transients actively chased off. To this repertoire I will add glocalization seen through the prism of marital relations. This metaphor speaks much more to the imagination than Roland Robertson's adaptive techniques of Japanese engineers. I would actually like to cite this entire entry from 2 February 2011, devoted to 'Glocalization attaining maturity'. But I will content myself with the formulation in these two sentences:

> 'Glocalization' is a name given to a marital cohabitation that has been obliged, despite all the sound and fury known only too well to the majority of wedded couples, to negotiate a bearable modus co-vivendi, as separation, let alone divorce, is neither a realistic nor a desirable option. Glocalization is a name for a love–hate relationship, mixing attraction with repulsion; love that lusts for proximity, mixed with hate that yearns for distance.[18]

Glocalization – you add – is the name of a relation of the type *Hassliebe*, a mixture of attraction and repulsion: a love yearning for closeness and a distaste fantasizing about distance. I think that if teachers, having studied many thick tomes written on globalization – including Roland Robertson's impressive, multi-volume *Encyclopedia of Globalization* – still had some difficulties with this concept, particularly with its relationship to local problems, they have now become somewhat smarter, and maybe for them it will also be a great help in their understanding of a world that increasingly evades comprehension.

So maybe, together, we are on the road to a greater understanding and increased ability to handle the world, because dialogue allows us to cross the boundaries of our own loneliness? That you are able to read newspapers, react to questions sent from different parts of the world, always reading new texts and finding in them accurate diagnoses of our reality allows me to believe that an alternative exists; that TINA (*There Is No Alternative*), proclaimed by Margaret Thatcher with such conviction and with such devastating results – not only for British society – is passing into the dustbin of history as one of the twentieth century's stupidest utterances by a politician. And that is good news.

ZB Well yes, two faiths – two mutually exclusive claims of monopoly on truth. Two monotheisms, as two stags locking antlers in the hope that the other will bend first and give way. Or, if you prefer, another one of those famed American duels, where the loser is whichever of the two drivers rushing towards a head-on collision, who turns chicken and gets out of his opponent's way.

But, to the aid of those numerous people who lack the stag's instinct or have no interest in taking part in American duels comes our great philosopher Cezary Wodziński in a short, ostensibly comic but in fact bitterly serious, discussion of a world divided, allegedly without remainder, into 'atheists' and 'anti-atheists', published in issue 48 of *Tygodnik Powszechny* under the title of 'Poza' (In Addition To): 'I suspect that the ones cannot survive without the others. And perhaps more: that they care only about themselves – in an opposition indistinguishable from a passionate embrace of two oppositionists in one position [...]'.[19] Wodziński makes a plea for those people for whom – as for him – there is no place in that prospectless head-scrapping, or who have no desire to join in the brawl. There are many such people – though not too many. Studies show that most of us find life without faith hard to accept, and even harder to practice. It is from this state of affairs that both varieties of monotheism, the 'scientific' and the 'theistic', draw their hope of victory and the determination to continue with hostilities – the sole result being the chances of an end to conflict growing yet more remote. This conflict looks as unavoidable as it is vain. The truths of philosophers are one thing, the truths of being-in-the-world quite another: unable to get rid of its paradoxes, deaf to the teachings of logicians and all in all intractable.

I repeat what I have said before: if God dies, it will only be together with humanity. And I base my expectations on the immortality of the human enchantment by beliefs that claim fullness and monopoly on truth. '[T]he road to a greater understanding and increased ability to handle the world' that you mention requires an understanding of this duality of the human condition – even if there are not many signs on heaven or earth that its widespread, let alone universal, acceptance is on the cards.

SO   Yes, the text of Cezary Wodziński's that you refer to deserves a closer and deeper look. Although the author of 'Poza' acknowledges a debt to Athens in his way of breaking apart words and ideas, linked to a lively distaste for accepting apparent reality, I perceive inspiration from beyond Athens. Maybe even from the Far East. But one should ask him directly about that. In the meantime, I would like to bring up my own experiences of the past few years which, perhaps, offer a possibility of escape from, or even winning out over, the locking of antlers that you describe.

For the last few years I have been participating in a seminar with professors and students from the Oriental Institute at the University of Warsaw. I very much regret that these lectures and discussions are not accessible to the broader public. They therefore remain the experience of a passing moment. But, despite this fleeting nature, something, of course, remains. At least for me, they are a form of intellectual and spiritual therapy, allowing me to untangle some of the knots of human history. Some of them appear to be Gordian knots, which can only be untangled with a radical cut. Meanwhile, reflection on texts written in all kinds of languages (we jokingly refer to our meetings as reversing the curse of Babel, because here no language is a barrier to understanding) illuminates their surprising kinship. It is amazing how texts, particularly those seen as sacred and which have so dominated our culture and religion, do not have to divide us, but quite the opposite: they should bring us together, because they mutually supplement and enlighten, and their explanations do not require political or forcible support. Do not worry Zygmunt, I will not judge these meetings, or torment you with memories of countless texts. Nonetheless, stimulated by this image of interlocked antlers, I will make reference to the most recent of them, which adopted precisely an alternative perspective on the historical divisions that have arisen over time. Insofar as I correctly understood the voices and intentions of the participants of this meeting, understanding is not only possible, but actually necessary, and this in light of those analysed texts. The point here is not understanding 'beyond' or 'above' those divisions, but within them. The point of departure for the main speaker, the Sinologist Zbigniew Słupski, was a text (delivered several months earlier in the same cluster of meetings) by M. Krzysztof Byrski, currently one of the greatest Polish scholars of the religious traditions of Hinduism and Buddhism, entitled

'Manifold Visions of the Meaning of Existence: the Spiritual Lega-
cies of the Bharata and Abraham', but the reasoning was based
on the teachings of Confucius, whom I will refer to in a moment.
In any case, in this lecture Byrski called for a renunciation of
dogmatic thinking and praised eclecticism and religious syncretism. And he found followers in the titular Bharata and adherents
of religions emerging from Abraham (Judaism, Christianity and
Islam). Thus, the Vedas, along with the Bible and the Qu'ran, if
they are read seriously and in keeping with the thinking of their
authors, are not in competition, but supplement each other. Byrski
is so deeply convinced of the mutual connections between Hinduism and Christianity (similar ideas about the creation of the world,
strongly related concepts of a sacrifice that has a redemptive character) that he does not see anything incongruous in regarding
Hinduism (which precedes Christianity chronologically) as an
earlier incarnation of divinity in history. From this comes the
straightforward conclusion that the belief in Jesus' mystical body,
so dear to Christianity, can be expanded to all of humankind. And
the fundamental justification of this conclusion, so shocking to
many Christians (but probably not to Hindus), is the idea both
traditions share, of God's sacrifice.

But the real alternative to opponents whose antlers are locked
in a death-match (incidentally I saw this kind of battle between
stags in a film made by foresters in the Puszcza Borecka (Borecka
Forest); one died, and the one who survived could not untangle
his antlers from the other's; it was only thanks to the help of a
forester that he was spared from sharing the fate of his opponent)
can be found, it seems to me, in the vision of Confucius. In Professor Słupski's lectures, at least, the Confucian tradition makes possible a peaceful victory over all divisions in worldview or religion.
For the Chinese sage, it is existence itself that merits interest; he
sees conflicts over its meaning as irrelevant, similarly to the debate
over his divinity. He does not shy away from ideas central to
various religions, such as love, or the good, but they bring him
into a positive relationship to another person. The basis of love
understood in this way is empathy, understanding and fellow-
feeling. It is concretely manifested in honest relationships to other
people, credibility, and in the choice of action that is most appropriate to a given situation. Thus, for Confucius, transcendence is
not important, but rather that which is accessible to people: the

experience of the consequences of our actions in the here and now. In Słupski's opinion, it is in such a perspective on the world that we must seek the source of Confucius' silence on the topic of transcendence, and treatment of religion as a strictly private affair. It is not surprising, then, that it is not the divine, but the other person, who is the source of wisdom. In this sense, the Chinese sage did not pass on a wisdom that was secretly transmitted to him, but renewed it and passed it on precisely through contacts with real people.

It seems to me that this view of religion and faith has very modern features; they are individualized and emerge from everyone's experience. They are various and incomparable. I personally perceive connections with Ulrich Beck's concept of a personal God, which we discussed earlier. Confucius allows us to look at the mutual interrelationship between theism and atheism in a new way. He takes the antagonistic edge off of that perspective. Does this situate us beyond? I don't think so; rather it places us at the very heart of existence. These thoughts were inspired by the most recent meeting of our 'Tower of Babel'. Other meetings were just as interesting. Currently there is much discussion in Poland about religion in schools and its status as a subject. If it was taught from such a broad cultural perspective, it could even be on the *matura* [the leaving exam for Polish high school students], and perhaps more students would decide to continue their studies at one of many Orientalist departments, and religion would not be associated with primitive catechisms, which effectively frighten people away.

But it is not only these seminars that make new perspectives on the meeting of theism and atheism possible. Not so long ago, Samuel Sandler, who is preparing an anniversary publication of Bolesław Prus' *Chronicles*, pointed out to me this fragment, written over 100 years ago:

Religion must be cultivated as the greatest treasure, the strongest motor of civilization; however, it must be true religion, not dead texts but living feelings and useful deeds, which are also lofty. True religion gives power to the will, peace to the heart, wings to the intellect. Instead of Inquisition it stands for tolerance; instead of divisions, compassion; instead of curses, blessings. It does not persecute those of different faiths, because it understands that different creeds are only various paths leading to one God. It does not enter into polemics with science, because it does not doubt that, sooner or later, science will confirm the most important truths of faith.[20]

From what I remember, Prus was not particularly pious, and tended to seek the sources of human happiness in science and the development of civilization. But this is precisely why this Positivist perceived the value of religion in such a modern way. I admit that, from my readings of contemporary texts on religion, in books whose subject is precisely the discussion of these recognized dimensions of each of them, I am starting to believe that it is possible to overcome these tensions. Well, maybe that is enough of books, because even without them we know, as you rightly remind us, that 'if God dies, it will only be together with humanity'. Before this happens, however, it is worth looking more closely at the increasingly many signs on earth that seem to be postponing this funeral.

ZB   So Byrski speaks to Słupski, Słupski ponders what he hears, Obirek listens intently to both and draws judicious conclusions from his reflections on what he hears; and all of them praise the self-restraint of Confucius and follow his example of suspending (for the duration of the conversation at least) such matters as cannot be reconciled to the benefit of issues that wink to each other – while staying aloof from the powder barrel widely known under the name of the 'struggle for truth': that fight for the monopoly on correctness and the right to ignore what others consider to be right.

What can be said apart from that such a stance is beautiful, wise and praiseworthy because of auguring well for human community; but how many people attend the seminars of the Orientalist Department of Warsaw University? Somewhat (somewhat?!) more numerous are, and probably will be for a foreseeable future, people who keenly lend their ears to Father Rydzyk's pronouncements proclaiming the Satanic provenance of everything lacking the Church's imprimatur; or else listen with rapt attention to the assertions of the ayatollahs while devoutly ingesting the lessons of mullahs who remind them in every other sentence that Allah is one and Mohammed is his prophet; or else remind themselves in a chorus several times daily, in prayer after prayer, that 'shma

Israel, Adonai elohejnu Adonai ehad' (Hear, O Israel: the Lord our God, the Lord is one)? And all of them, these more numerous ones, do it not with the aim of breaking down borders and divisions, or in the name of Gadamer's fusion of horizons, but out of concern for a better fortification of the frontiers and more vigilant border guards, and for reducing yet further the already scant border traffic of the faithful. Speaking plainly: they crave *anathemism* rather than *ecumenism*, seeking exclusion rather than union.

Which does not mean that you are not correct, Staszek, when you surmise that 'it is possible to overcome these tensions' (though I am not sure that 'increasingly many signs on earth' attest to this). There is no lack of philosophical recipes for overcoming tensions (I can mention, for instance, Kołakowski's praise of inconsistency, or Odo Marquard's *Abschied vom Prinzipiellen*, or Ulrich Beck's aforementioned cosmopolitan crusade, or the tripartite formula of Richard Sennett); what is more, the objective but eternally kaleidoscopically shifting and changeable human condition, under the influence of the unceasing diasporization of the planet, is clearly approaching (though not without obstacles and resistance) the model postulated by Confucius (in which, as you say, 'transcendence is not important, but rather that which is accessible to people: the experience of the consequences of our actions in the here and now'; he says little about transcendence but treats faith as 'strictly private' – 'It is not surprising, then, that it is not the divine, but the other person, who is the source of wisdom') – although people finding themselves in this new condition are, to put it mildly, exceedingly slow to realize it (to say nothing of deriving from it pragmatic, correct conclusions about the world). Consciousness is regularly delayed in catching up with a change of conditions; anthropologists even have a term for this drawback: 'cultural lag'. For consciousness to catch up to the condition requires time. It would be difficult to reflect a new condition in consciousness before its contours are clearly drawn – that is, before its mental 'articulation'. That latter task falls to 'professional thinkers'.

In *Legislators and Interpreters*, following the observations of the American anthropologist Paul Radin, I tried to trace their convoluted road from 'primitive philosophers' onwards. According to Radin, in 'primitive societies' it is already possible to distinguish between two general temperaments: that of the priest-intellectual and that of the layman. The first is only loosely linked to action and focuses on fathoming the nature of religious phenomena, whereas the second is first and foremost concerned with practical action, and is in some sense a derivative of the first type's accomplishments. But even in that distant time, Radin observed and documented, in a fundamental text published in 1937 and entitled *Primitive Religion: Its Nature and Origin*, a phenomenon that even today persists in the foundations of (all) religion: 'Primitive man is afraid of one thing, of the uncertainties of the struggle of life'[21] – and it is from this widely experienced uncertainty that the priest-intellectual derives his general vision of the dangers of the world and specific ways to overcome them, thus establishing the core of both ancient and the most recent religious beliefs. I do not know whether it was under the influence of reading Radin, but a very similar concept of the origins and function of religion was developed by Mikhail Bakhtin in his theory of recasting the 'cosmic fear' into an 'official fear'[22] – and also in Leszek Kołakowski, who sought the sources of religion in fears stemming from the intellectual and practical inadequacy of humankind.

If we accept this conception, it would be reasonable to expect two seemingly contradictory pronouncements from priest-intellectuals of all ages: 'Be afraid!' and 'Rid yourselves of fear!' The first message adds weight to the second – adding by the same token importance and attractiveness to the specific prescription for freedom from fear which the second message offers. The former message deepens an already present need for the latter – but does not determine its contents. The contents can be, and are, quite varied. And if the first message is common to all forms of religion, including the Bharata and the Abrahamic, the second is at the core of the multiplicity of its variations, and the conflicts between them. The first is – potentially – a fertile soil for ecumenism; the second clears the site for anathemist practices. But I share your view that they do not foreclose the possibility of visualizing the Tower of Babel turning from curse into blessing. And I agree that the Orientalist seminar at UW is worthy of being popularized and emulated as an attempt to do that work, so indispensable for the future of humankind – because the contents of the second message are split into two categories, one redeeming and the other catastrophic for humanity, one nurturing human solidarity and the other feeding hostility and aggression.

SO   Well, you have poured such cold rain on my parade, though at least you raised the temperature slightly by acknowledging the merit of, and need for, such elite activities as our university seminar. It is true that its warmth benefits only a small handful of enthusiasts and devoted readers of texts from far-flung parts of the world, who in no way rival the number of followers of Father Rydzyk and other fiery speakers of truths that are in no way of the collective, but actually strive for division. You are correct in your observation that preachers, mullahs and rabbis who act 'out of concern for a better fortification of the frontiers and more vigilant border guards, and for reducing yet further the already scant border traffic of the faithful', find many more sympathetic ears than philological worker-bees encouraging people to read the texts. Finding points of contact is not as emotionally absorbing and fascinating as finding and highlighting differences. Already, in one of our first conversations, you pointed me towards Fredric Barth's wise observation on the sources of difference. I think it is worthwhile to mention it once more in this new context (the strivings of 'dialogians' and 'anathemists') – particularly because you mentioned it almost as if you disagreed, but for me it was and continues to be inspiring. In your lecture, *New Frontiers and Universal Values*, given in Barcelona in 2004, you referred to Fredric Barth and quoted his words on the subject of frontiers. You said that 'borders are not drawn to separate differences. It is exactly the other way round. It is because we have drawn the border that we actively seek differences and become acutely aware of their presence. Differences are the product of borders, of the activity of separation',[23] and added 'First the border is drawn and then people start looking for the justification of this border being put in this place, and then differences on two sides of the border are noted; they acquire enhanced significance, since they justify the border and explain why it should be kept intact.'[24] In other words, the function of the intellectual – regardless of whether we follow Paul Radin in seeing him as a practical person or view him as a religious one only serving the world of ideas – comes down to legitimizing the doings of others: politicians, religious leaders or other rulers of the world. Of course, there is no lack of solitary wanderers, such as you mention – Kołakowski, Beck, Sennett, Bakhtin and Radin – who try to strike out in new directions. They rouse us from habitual ways of seeing and jolt us into adapting to a new understanding of the complexities of this world. Each of them in their own way, because they had to overcome different challenges. Each of them is close to me; I feel a kinship with them and a great sense of indebtedness, and their reflections allow me to believe that mine are not due to a herd instinct, but solitary grappling with the meaning of my existence.

I will try not to dismiss these warnings which you mentioned above, which are reasonable and in every way just, but also to develop somewhat optimistic accents, justifying to some extent reflections that are not fully to be consigned to the discussions of philologists. This time I will allow myself to direct your attention, Zygmunt, to an author who has very much interested me for several years, and continues to ever more strongly. I am speaking of an excellent scholar of the Talmud and Hebrew Bible, who for some time now has taken an interest in Christianity and the Christian way of looking at the world. As it seems to me, the books of this author are an example of the crossing of boundaries described by Barth, and indicate a direction for, and possibility of, overcoming them. I am speaking of Daniel Boyarin, for whom both Jesus of Nazareth and Paul of Tarsus are spokesmen of Judaism, and their learning is contained within the framework of that religion. I believe that he convincingly demonstrates how today's anthropology shows us the arbitrariness of the division between Judaism and Christianity. In his newest book, *The Jewish Gospels: the Story of Jesus Christ*, Boyarin writes: 'If there is one thing that Christians know about their religion, it is that it is not Judaism. If there is one thing that Jews know about their religion, it is that it is not Christianity.'[25] This sharp awareness of the difference between two religions is the product of enormous efforts by Jews and Christians to draw boundaries in the first century of our era. Christian theologians and rabbis were the most active in this task, and how their efforts looked and why they put so much effort into emphasizing their mutual differences is the subject of Boyarin's book, which deserves serious consideration. In my opinion, it should be required reading for both Christians and Jews – and maybe for anyone who wants to understand what happens to any religion when it begins to fall under the sway of non-religious forces. I will cite a passage from the third chapter, 'Jesus kept kosher':

> Most (if not all) of the ideas and practices of the Jesus movement of the first century and the beginning of the second century – and even later – can be safely understood as part of the ideas and practices that we understand to be the Judaism of this period. The ideas of Trinity and incarnation, or certainly the germs of those ideas, were already present among Jewish believers well before Jesus came on the scene to incarnate them in himself [...] according to the Gospel of Mark, Jesus kept kosher, which is to say that he saw himself not as abrogating the Torah but as defending it. There was controversy with some other Jewish leaders as to how best to observe the Law, but none, I will argue, about *whether* to observe it. According to Mark (and Matthew even more so), far from abandoning the laws and practices of the Torah, Jesus was a staunch defender of the Torah.[26]

If I am not exhausting your patience, I will note one more book by Boyarin, *Border Lines: the Partition of Judeo-Christianity*, which discusses a fascinating image of the gradual distancing between these two religions.[27] As he himself admits, 'In this book, I am suggesting that the borders between Judaism and Christianity have been historically constructed out of acts of discursive (and too often actual) violence, especially acts of violence against heretics who embody the instability of our constructed essences.'[28] It is precisely the determination of how these borderlines came to be drawn, and the identification of the primary architects of this task, that is the fundamental goal of *Border Lines*. If one looks attentively at the sources of Christianity, it clearly emerges that, from its very beginnings, it was deeply interested in seeking out its own identity, and the most important lesson that contributed to this was 'heresy-ology', or an ability to identify heresy and heretics. Its essence led to the division and labelling of those Christians who did not fit 'inside', or within the framework of orthodoxy, which was of course delimited by the Christian theologians themselves. And important portions of such 'heretics' were 'Jews, or more precisely Judaizers'. They were seen as an example of hybrids or true 'monstra', as one of the early Church Fathers, Ignatius of Antioch, called them. In his opinion, 'It is monstrous to talk of

Jesus Christ and to practice Judaism.'[29] The rabbis had an analo-
gous reaction when writing about the unclean, the infected, hybrids
called *min*, or all those who, in their thinking, approached an
increasingly hated and feared Christianity. Thus, in Boyarin's
opinion, boundaries were historically constructed through an act
of discursive violence (and sometimes through physical violence),
and the process of demarcating them caused both sides to suffer.
One of the main elements of these delineated boundaries was a
concept of orthodoxy and, closely correlated with it, was a concept
of heresy. Both were created and described by 'heresiologists'
guarding the gates of orthodoxy. And in the efforts of both Church
Fathers and rabbis, aiming for the clarification of differences
between Judaism and Christianity, heresiology played a key role.
In other words both Judaism and Christianity are ideological
constructs devised in order to satisfy specific needs. Whether these
needs were religious or not, I am not sure.

Will Boyarin, along with Byrski and Słupski, share the fate
of these solitary combatants fighting to defeat the curse of Babel?
It is hard to say – though I fear that there are more and more
signs on earth to indicate that this is exactly what will happen. I
trust, however, that this is yet another return of my own pessi-
mism, which will eventually be conquered by events that do not
confirm it.

ZB I attempted to grapple with these problems years ago in
Modernity and Ambivalence. And I came then to the conclusion
that the closer the two sides of conflict are, the more virulently
they will struggle against each other (we spoke of this earlier,
calling on Mary Douglas' *Purity and Danger* and Edmund Leach's
essays for support). Heretics are more hideous enemies than
pagans, reformers than unbelievers, lukewarm followers than
opponents throwing off all disguises. And how rightly you point
out that 'Judaizers' are more threatening than self-declared Jews.
Ignatius of Antioch knew very well what he was saying: the most
intolerable – because the most threatening to the right worldview
and identity – are those (often countless!) people who straddle the
boundaries, seeking out similarities rather than differences, viewing
borders as provisional and building bridges where there ought to
be walls and trenches. 'Agreers', they are chidingly and disparag-
ingly called, and their fate is banishment or the death penalty.

Boyarin's reasoning, I think, is even more despicable and unacceptable to the guardians of fortified temples than the spokesmen of doctrines that are resolutely, openly and aggressively antagonistic. The latter confirm the guardians of purity's view of the world order and the infrangibility of identity – which the former dilute and erode. The latter foster alertness; the former lull to rest. Ultimately, the latter add weight to the issue, which the former sap or play down. Ambivalence is the deadly enemy of borders. And borders are drawn, fortified, manned with guards armed-to-the-teeth to combat the ambivalence; or at least to empty the sting of ambivalence of its venom before chasing it out of sight or casting it into oblivion.

Jesus and Mary were Jews – this is a fact that cannot be concealed or denied; one can, however, try, not necessarily unsuccessfully, to strip that fact of its meaning, by pronouncing that it is 'a monstrosity to talk of Jesus Christ and practice Judaism' – and thus the impossibility of reconciling those two activities after the Jews who resolved to continue Judaist practices gave Christ up to die. This is how unbearable, ambivalence-spawning 'and... and' monsters/hybrids/ mutants, are replaced by 'either...or', or those pure-bred in their distinct modalities. This procedure heralded the end of negotiations – bah, it made further negotiations pointless.

Considering the polycentric, polyglot and (yes!) polytheistic state of our world, it is hard for me to share the hopes that you place in Boyarin's assertions. They will not lead to the reconciliation of monotheisms, or of churches guarding their own sovereignty (about whether they do so out of 'religious needs', I am as dubious as you are...). Boyarin's line of reasoning (directed towards inveterate similarities and convergence) tends inevitably towards questioning the independent identities of two protagonists – and thus one should expect that it will be resolutely, angrily dismissed by both. Boyarin brings back from its exile, as your reading suggests, the monster of ambivalence, on whose exorcism both sides had worked for centuries, to a large degree resting on it their self-definition and self-determination. By the same token, Boyarin threatens to make null and void the effort in which they invested their hopes for the security of their sovereignty and of (to use Paul Ricoeur's distinction) both 'l'ipseité' and 'le mêmeté' of their identity.

For the same reasons that emerged in the previous paragraph, I place more hope in strivings in another direction, taking a long detour so as to avoid mutual revisions of identity – the road that leads through respect for self-definition, and understanding of (though not necessarily agreement with) the motives (and also the necessities emerging from a situation) that propelled it; something like that which Sennett perceived when creating his tripartite formula of humanism in a world divided into diasporas, or the ideas of Habermas, in his propagation of 'constitutional patriotism' fostering the group loyalties of diasporas. I see this route as much more sensible from a pragmatic perspective, but also as much more morally sound. Because, as Levinas would probably agree, moral responsibility for the other also encompasses (in some circumstances, and mainly!) responsibility for his/her right to self-determination and recognition of the identity s/he chooses.

In brief: I am in favour of efforts to persuade conflicting Churches and their congregations to accept the principle that, from the conviction that God is one, it does not follow that a person cannot imagine Him in various ways and worship him in various ways; to persuade them (in keeping with the logic of human relations) that adopting this principle will grant the God they worship glory and power, instead of making him the subject of bargaining and wrestling, as he is now.

Can you find a more humanitarian formula for the co-existence of monotheisms in an incurably polytheistic world?!

VII

God or Gods? The Gentle Face of Polytheism

Stanisław Obirek   It is hard to find a formula, and the ones proposed in the past do not seem to me to have been particularly successful. I am not in a hurry to propose new ones, though it is perhaps worth remembering the ones that strive to reconcile water and fire, and it is certainly worthwhile to become acquainted with these various attempts. But before I say a few words about this, I must admit that you rather burst my balloon, unveiling the dark side of my hero Daniel Boyarin by perceiving the drawbacks to his efforts to reconcile two embattled sides. Although unwillingly, I must concede your claim that he evokes strong feelings. Why mince words? He infuriates, and is unlikely to find fans, among either Christians or Jews; quite the opposite, some see him as a crypto-Christian, others as the fifth column of Judaism, and no explanation will help. His last book about Jesus met with a particularly harsh reception, with claims that it was derivative of other scholarship, and that the parts that were original were simply incorrect. I, of course, do not agree with such vicious judgments, and I think that Boyarin is a courageous man who impinges on the positive self-regard of entrenched experts on heresies of all kinds.

Another such brave man openly advocating polytheism met a similar fate. I have referenced him already in another context, praising his insightful analyses of cultural memory from ancient

Egypt to the present day. I am of course speaking of Jan Assmann, whose books on the Egyptians of Moses' time espied an opportunity in polytheism, and pointed out the disastrous consequences of the introduction of monotheism, linking it to 'Mosaic distinction'. He saw the greatest sin of this differentiation as being the impossibility of 'translating' one God into other gods; his predatory and jealous singularity condemned other gods – if not into non-existence, then to a temporary and constantly threatened being. The unheard-of novelty of this idea, and its tragic consequences, derived from the way it ended the free flow of ideas and gods from one civilization to another. Depending on the possibilities (not necessarily religious), various gods took control over souls and minds. But this single one was not willing to take part in any trades or translations. This new God stood for a radical newness – he proposed a non-negotiable road in one direction. As Assmann demonstrated in his long and persuasive exposés, polytheism did not die a natural death. It resurfaced and made its existence known, even in Christian Europe, where examples of it can be seen particularly clearly in the Renaissance, the philosophy of Spinoza, and the Enlightenment. In modern times, Sigmund Freud came to its aid, striving to clear Jews of the charge of introducing monotheism. Although Assmann explained that he writes not as a theologian, but as an Egyptologist and anthropologist, this did not help at all when he came under attack from apologists for monotheism, who launched increasingly serious accusations and series of criticisms at the audacious scholar.

In brief, his thesis evoked such violent opposition that the author felt compelled to write another book, this time concentrating on the price that humanity had to pay for the introduction of monotheism, returning to the same questions as before. As you can easily guess, he not only did not convince the convinced monotheists, he enraged them all the more. It is not for me to judge who is right in this case, but rather I will repeat the wisdom of Leszek Kołakowski, whom we both hold dear, who said that it is not the resolution of the conflict that is of importance, but the existence of two sides, even mutually exclusive ones, which adds vigour to our culture. In my opinion, he summoned enough interesting proofs of this for them to be worth not only remembering, but also referencing in the context of our conversation. Among the voices criticizing Assmann's thesis, we must mention Joseph

Ratzinger, who, as the deputy of the Congregation for the Doctrine of Faith, was avidly tracking signs of unorthodoxy.[1] It is probably due to his effectiveness in defending the Catholic Church's sole claim to truth that he was chosen to be Pope in 2005. An apologia for polytheism was a particularly irritating and bothersome historical truth for Ratzinger. In his view, and probably not only his, it was not monotheism that launched conflict between religious people, but polytheism that caused unending rivalries, and a multiplicity of gods that urged their followers on to a mutual 'convincing each other' of the superiority of their heavenly beings, often leading to physical force and violent opposition. What was most important in the assertions of this (former) Pope was that monotheism, particularly the monotheism manifested in Jesus Christ, is the one and truest truth, and all other religions are merely weaker presentiments, unclear traces. I perceived an echo of the declaration 'Dominus Iesus' proclaimed in 2000 by this very Ratzinger, in which he announced quite unambiguously the truth 'On the Unicity and Salvific Universality of Jesus Christ and the Church'. For the believers, then, there is nothing new in this argument. But the very fact of such a concerted opposition to other ways of looking at the past is, to me, yet another proof of the weakness of monotheism, rather than of its strength. Because, after all, supporters of polytheism in no way want to fight their monotheistic adversaries; rather, they demand a right to existence and to express their own vision of religion. Is that so much to ask? And, above all, for God's sake, whom does it harm? Probably not God? And what to do with atheists, for whom neither polytheism nor monotheism is appealing? It seems to me that we need a new way of looking at the problem, but how should we view it?

I saved the best for last; a voice and proposition that is receiving increasing acclaim. One of my American friends, Peter C. Phan, a phenomenal theologian of Vietnamese ancestry who lectures at Georgetown, the Jesuit university in Washington, has for years been arguing for the possibility of reconciling obeisance to multiple religions, which in no way contradicts belonging to the Catholic Church. Indeed, he was even able to defend his position in a spat with the aforementioned Vatican Congregation for the Doctrine of Faith. I frequently rely on his texts, especially on the book in which he delineated this stance in a particularly clear way[2] – because Asia was and is a testament to the ability of multiple religions to co-exist in a peaceful way. It was the intrusion of the West (Christianity and Islam in particular) that disturbed this harmony and taught the Asians to attack each other for their religious differences. We are familiar with descriptions of the shock experienced by Christian missionaries who were rudely surprised to encounter inhabitants of India respectfully placing figures of Mary and Joseph on their family altars alongside their own gods. The people in India did not see any problems with doing so; indeed, they did it with full respect for the differences between them. Today, even there, things are different, though who knows whether Asia will return to its roots and remind itself of more than Confucius? In any case, I look in that direction with great hope, and with a sense of possibility, rather than danger.

Zygmunt Bauman   Here, then, we have met in agreement – after playing, so many times, unwillingly but unavoidably (forced by the awareness of the peculiarities of our respective situations and their constraints) – 'devils' advocates': advocates of apparently two different devils – complementary, nevertheless, in their joint assistance of one devil in his two differing incarnations.

   We were both driven by the same desire to reconcile the multiplicity of religions with the oneness of humanity: to discover or compose – for a universally shared human benefit – a practical resolution of the paradox of humanity sentenced simultaneously to the unity of its fate and a diversity of ways of perceiving it and experiencing it. We were prompted to do so through compiling an inventory and a map of the traps and ambushes by which each one of the found/invented resolutions cannot but be besieged: unable to wish/argue/conjure them away, we tried at least to increase, somewhat, the odds of evading them. We have arrived, guided by you, to Peter Phan: to solutions that have survived till this day here and there in the regions of Asia, far from Europe, but were practised a long time ago on the territory of the Roman Empire, which holds the record of longevity among multi-ethnic, multi-religious and multi-lingual human agglomerates. Edward Gibbon, in *The History of the Decline and Fall of the Roman Empire*, picked up the proclamation of Christianity as the one and mandatory state religion as the cause of the demise of the centuries-long peaceful cohabitation of races, tribes and cultures, and so of the Roman Empire and Pax Romana. One of the reasons (arguably the paramount among them) of the unique durability of both was allowing every household between Hadrian's Wall and the Persian border its own Lares and Penates, and all and any of them to worship any god chosen at will from the all-Empire Pantheon.

'Dark times', as Hannah Arendt described them, 'are not only not new, they are no rarity in history'.[3] It often happened, as Arendt points out, borrowing a phrase of Heidegger's, that 'das Licht der Öffentlichkeit verdunkelt alles' (the light of the public obscures everything), and then 'illumination may well come less from theories and concepts than from the uncertain, flickering, and often weak light that some men and women, in their lives and works, will kindle under almost all circumstances'.[4] In this sense, we live today, once more, in 'dark times'. Arendt saw Gotthold Ephraim Lessing, the pioneer of the German Enlightenment, as an example of a philosopher of 'dark times' – and she did so for a variety of reasons. One of them was his acknowledgment of 'openness to others' as a base requirement of humanism: 'truly human dialogue differs from mere talk or even discussion in that it is entirely permeated by pleasure in the other person and what he says'.[5] Another was the conviction that harm to human society comes not from those who – as indeed Lessing himself – 'take more trouble to make clouds than to scatter them', but from those 'who wish to subject all men's ways of thinking to the yoke of their own'.[6] Lessing's thought, Arendt writes, was not, as in Plato, a conversation 'between me and myself', but an 'anticipation of dialogue with others' – a type of thought that 'needs no pillars and props'[7] (which, by the way, typically turned out to be the pillars of political systems and props of coercion). But the primary reason to name Lessing as a prototypical 'philosopher of dark times' was the fact that he rejoiced in the very things that have ever – or at least since Parmenides and Plato – distressed philosophers:

> that the truth, as soon as it is uttered, is immediately transformed into one opinion among many, is contested, reformulated, reduced to one subject of discourse among others. Lessing's greatness does not merely consist in a theoretical insight that there cannot be one single truth within the human world but in his gladness that it does

not exist and that, therefore, the unending discourse among men
will never cease so long as there are men at all.[8]

For Lessing (and with Arendt's full agreement), in other words,
the end of contention would be tantamount to the end of humanity. Everything creative in human existence, creative in its very
nature of humanity and its inalienable essence, has its roots in
human diversity. And it is not human diversity that turns into
brother killing brother – but its rejection and the intention to have
it one's own way, at whatever cost. The preliminary condition of
peace, solidarity and benevolent cooperation among humans is
consent to the multiplicity of ways of being human and willingness
to accept the model of co-existence that such multiplicity requires.

But the final word in our – for me, quite eye-opening – conversation belongs to you, my sure-footed guide through a terrain
previously known to me only from hearsay... Thus I await it just
as impatiently as I awaited each of your previous consecutive
challenges.

SO Zygmunt, do you remember our first meeting in Kraków in
the Alley of Doubting Thomas, when I succeeded in convincing
you to write an essay for the quarterly *Spiritual Life*, entitled
'What Do Non-believers Believe In (and Are There Any?)'? There
you wrote – and we on the Editorial Board noticed your wise
diagnoses with interest – 'The point is not that people are losing
faith in eternal values, stepping beyond the horizon of the passing
moment. The issue is, rather, that *eternity, for a normal citizen of
the market-consumerist world, has ceased to be a value.*'[9] And you
added:

> People worried over how, from the crumbling ore of actions and
> accomplishments of a butterfly-like fleetingness, a noble metal of
> eternity could be forged. This eternal struggle is called 'culture' by
> some; others, more abstractly, call it 'transcendence' – but it works
> out to be the same thing. Every culture has busied itself with the
> creation of ladders, which its adherents could climb so as to sur-
> mount the fate of mortal beings that has fallen to them. All cultures
> known to us were the workshops of alchemists, in which evanes-
> cence was re-imagined as eternal existence. A culture like ours, a
> market-consumerist one, a culture that makes fluidity its apotheosis

and dismisses anything that is unfit for immediate consumption, has never before existed.[10]

Your text has become an important reference point for many readers of the quarterly, though there were also those who criticized us for publishing texts by non-believers or seekers. I will mention only the crucial voices of Jan Woleński, Michał Głowiński and Stanisław Lem. All of them were included in the anthology, *What Connects Us? A Conversation with Non-believers*, which allowed Leszek Kołakowski to write in its introduction that 'it is a confrontation between faith and non-faith, a confrontation that is not only civilized, but is overall permeated with an intelligent desire to understand the other side'.[11]

For me personally, the experience became a pretext – first for giving a lecture at a conference devoted to European leaders, and later to publishing a text in which your writings were set alongside those of John Paul II. I will allow myself to refer to a fragment of this text, which it seems to me has not lost its relevance:

I would like to point to the consistent development of and loyalty to internal truth. One, as Pope, in 2003 published an apostolic exhortation called *Ecclesia in Europa*; the other, in 2005, a book: *Europe: an Unfinished Adventure*. *Ecclesia in Europa* is a kind of summation of John Paul II's concerns about Europe and its Christian legacy; *Europe: an Unfinished Adventure* is a witty reflection on the unpredictability of a continent, which for thousands of years stood for the world's development of civilization. One can certainly question the appropriateness of this juxtaposition. John Paul II's reflections emerge from a clearly delineated tradition of western Christianity, whereas Zygmunt Bauman's thoughts cannot be easily traced to any one source. One could even say that it is a programmatic distaste for any certainties. The only thing that unites them is concern for the poor. Is this little, or much? Naturally, Zygmunt Bauman has devoted his entire life to the possibility of conquering the aporia of social formations, finding an answer in socialist sensitivities, and since his early childhood Karol Wojtyła believed that religion is the most appropriate answer to the anxieties of the human heart. Gesturing towards a common denominator – sensitivity to poverty – I do not intend to suggest that the Pope is a socialist, or that Zygmunt Bauman is a religious thinker. But I do want to suggest that different points of departure do not need to mean an impossibility of meeting. I am emboldened to juxtapose them by the 25th chapter of the Gospel of St Matthew, where one criterion for an authentic life is concern for 'the least of these'.[12]

Thus we have agreed even earlier, and I see our eighteen attempts to persuade and explain to each other that an understanding is possible as a continuation of that earlier, still tentative, effort. Did we succeed in saying more this time? It is probably not for us to say. But for my part I can say that it was a great honour and intellectual feast for me, as well as a spiritual stimulus, to be able to read through your reactions and answers. I am grateful to you for bringing my thoughts to earth, pointing out blind spots and urging me towards other, less immediately visible directions.

For a long time I have been convinced that theology has much to learn from the sciences, if it would like to. The latter, especially in Poland, very tentatively suggest a possibility that the study of God could benefit from their services. I have a tentative hope that together we have succeeded in indicating points of convergence and an open ground where the two fields overlap. I trust that we did not do injury to theologians or to hard-working scientists. Perhaps it will not be too much for me to repeat the statement of retiring Roman senators (given that you made warm reference to the Roman Empire in your concluding remarks): 'feci, quod potui, faciant meliora potentes' (I have done what I could; let those who can do better). Given that Stanisław Lem left instructions that these words were to be carved on his tombstone, it is in no way a discredit to us to feel a connection to his way of thinking.

Without Conclusions

Stanisław Obirek   I leave this text open, in the hope that this lack of a conclusion speaks to its value. I personally believe that the main problem does not come down to the possibility of reconciling polytheism and monotheism, but to coming to terms with the fact that both forms of faith are merely efforts to describe one's place in the world. One of the fastest-growing groups in the world is 'nons', or people openly declaring a lack of interest in any form of religious belonging. In my view, this is good news for everyone, believers and non-believers, indicating an inadequacy of current forms of belonging. Maybe it is worth rethinking history, even the history of religion.

Inviting Zygmunt Bauman into a conversation about religion, I had hoped that he would confirm this optimism of mine. This is indeed what happened, for which I thank him from the bottom of my heart. I have the sense that we paused only for a moment. Maybe it was the moment of writing our texts, anticipating reactions, surprise that it was precisely this one and not a different one. Meanwhile, we both have the inescapable feeling that it could have been different. If we had read other books, met other people, experienced a different piece of history, our thinking would doubtless have gone in a different direction. Does this sense of arbitrariness and specific timeliness explain the limitations of our writings? It is not for us to judge, but it seems to me, paradoxically, that this is the strength of, and catalyst for, dialogue. Perhaps even the invitation not to stop with our writings, but to see them only as another stop on the road, whose endpoint is unknown to all. Did we succeed in unveiling the edges of the secrets of existence? Certainly not, but we were able to ask questions without fear of their consequences, without concerns about sanctions from those unwilling to entertain free thought. Some will certainly look for yet another aberration of postmodern liquidity and the lack of stable points of departure. If this inconclusiveness of thought provokes them into reflection on issues crucial to the people of today then our propositions will lead to a fortunate conclusion, precisely in these reactions. Whether we ourselves will be tempted to further pieces is a question for the future, which we cannot predict. We are left with uncertainty – the mother of freedom and moral decisions.

Zygmunt Bauman   Amen.

Notes

I Preliminary Measures

1 Maciej Zięba, *Nieznane, Niepewne, Niebezpieczne* ('Unknown, Unsure, Unsafe'). PIW: 2011, p. 58. Translations are by Katarzyna Bartoszynska, unless otherwise noted. NB: Although this text has not been translated into English, another work of Zieba's that addresses similar topics has been. See *Papal Economics: The Catholic Church on Democratic Capitalism, from* Rerum novarum *to* Caritas in veritate. ISI Books: 2013, especially the conclusion, 'From Centesimus annus to Caritas in veritate'.

2 Zięba, *Nieznane*, pp. 60–1.

3 Odo Marquard, *Abschied vom Prinzipiellen. Farewell to Matters of Principle: Philosophical Studies*. Translated by Robert M. Wallace with the assistance of Susan Bernstein and James I. Porter. Oxford University Press: 1989, p. 123.

4 Yochanan Muffs, *The Personhood of God: Biblical Theology, Human Faith and the Divine Image*. Woodstock: 2005, p. 99.

5 Ibid., p. 59.

6 Abraham Joshua Heschel, *God in Search of Man: A Philosophy of Judaism*. Farrar, Straus and Giroux: 1976.

7 Muffs, *Personhood*, p. 69.

8 Ibid., p. 94.

9 Israel Knohl, *The Divine Symphony: the Bible's Many Voices*. Jewish Publication Society: 2003, p. 8.

10 Ibid., p. 33.

11 Ibid., p. 143.
12 Here I am relying mainly on the following texts: Gershom Scholem, *Kabbalah*. Quadrangle: 1974; *Sabbatai Sevi, The Mystical Messiah*. Princeton University Press: 1973; *The Messianic Idea in Judaism*. Allen and Unwin: 1971.
13 Emmanuel Levinas, *Nine Talmudic Readings*. Indiana University Press: 1990, pp. 33–4.

II What about This Religion? On the Threat of Fundamentalism – Not Only the Religious Kind

1 Karen Armstrong, *A History of God: the 4,000-Year Quest of Judaism, Christianity and Islam*. Ballantine Books: 1994.
2 Moshe Idel, *Kabbalah: New Perspectives*. Yale University Press: 1990.
3 Moshe Idel, *Messianic Mystics*. Yale University Press: 1998.
4 Idel, *Kabbalah*, p. xvii.
5 Paul Veyne, *L'empire gréco-romain*. Seuil: 2008.
6 Johann Wolfgang von Goethe, *Faust*. Translated by Walter Kaufmann. Anchor Books: 1963, 1.7.1699–1700.
7 Primo Levi, *Survival in Auschwitz*. Translated by Giulio Einaudi. Touchstone Press: 1996, p. 29.
8 See Robert Putnam, *Bowling Alone: The Collapse and Revival of American Community*. Simon & Schuster: 2000.
9 Levinas, *Readings*, p. 47.
10 See David Campbell and Robert Putnam, *American Grace: How Religion Divides and Unites Us*. Simon & Schuster: 2010.
11 Leszek Kołakowski, *Co nas łączy? Dialog z niewierzącymi* ('What Connects Us? A Conversation with Non-believers'). WAM: 2002.

III The Literati in Aid of Blundering Thought

1 J. M. Coetzee, *Diary of a Bad Year*. Vintage: 2007, p. 83.
2 Ibid., p. 85.
3 It also has not been translated into English.

IV Sources of Hope

1 See Zygmunt Bauman, Roman Kubicki and Anna Zeidler-Janiszewska, *Życie a kontekstach* ('Life in Contexts'). Wydawnictwo Akademickie i Profesjonalne: 2009, pp. 154–5.

2 See J. M. Coetzee, *Diary of a Bad Year*. Vintage: 2007, p. 79.

3 José Saramago, *The Notebook*. Translated by Amanda Hopkinson and Daniel Hahn. Verso: 2010.

4 Ulrich Beck, *A God of One's Own: Religion's Capacity for Peace and Potential for Violence*. Polity: 2010, p. 156.

5 Odo Marquard, 'In Praise of Polytheism', in *Farewell to Matters of Principle: Philosophical Studies*. Oxford University Press: 1989, 87–110, p. 93.

6 Georg Christoph Lichtenberg, *The Waste Books*. Translated and with an Introduction by R. J. Hollingdale. New York Review Books: 2000, p. 44.

7 Hans-Georg Gadamer, *Truth and Method*. Translation revised by Joel Weinsheimer and Donal G. Marshall. Continuum: 2004, p. 289.

8 See ibid.

9 Ibid., p. 305.

10 See Citati, *Israele e l'Isla: le scintille di Dio* ('Israel and Islam: Divine Sparks'). Mondadori: 2003.

11 Ibid. ZB's translation.

12 Ibid. ZB's translation.

13 Ibid. ZB's translation.

V Fusion of Horizons

1 Amin Maalouf, *Les Identités meurtrières. In the Name of Identity: Violence and the Need to Belong*. Translated by Barbara Bray. Arcade Publishing: 2000.

2 Ibid., p. 51.

3 Citati, *Israele e l'Islam: le scintille di Dio* ('Israel and Islam: Divine Sparks'). Mondadori: 2003, pp. 176–7.

4 Ibid.

5 Ibid.

6 Ibid.

7 Joseph Roth, *Collected Shorter Fiction of Joseph Roth*. Translated by Michael Hofmann. Granta Books: 2001, pp. 250, 251.

8 Plato, *The Seventh Letter*. Translated by B. Jowett and J. Harward. Encyclopedia Britannica: 1952.

9 Plato. *Phaedrus*. Translated by Benjamin Jowett. Clarendon Press: 1892, p. 75.

10 Ibid., p. 76.

11 Wiesław Myśliwski, 'Kres kultury chłopskiej' (The End of Peasant Culture), *Twórczość* ('Works'), 4/701 (April 2004), p. 53.

12 Ibid., p. 56.
13 Ibid., p. 57.

VI   The Disinherited; or, Creating Tradition Anew

1 Jack Goody, *The Logic of Writing and the Organization of Society*. Cambridge University Press: 1986.
2 Ibid., pp. 102–3.
3 Ibid., p. 10.
4 Ibid., pp. 9–10.
5 Jan Assmann, *Cultural Memory and Early Civilization: Writing, Remembrance, and Political Imagination*. Cambridge University Press: 2011, p. 187.
6 Ibid., p. 4.
7 Zygmunt Bauman, *Legislators and Interpreters: On Modernity, Post-Modernity and Intellectuals*. Polity: 1989.
8 Carlo Ginzburg, *The Cheese and the Worms: the Cosmos of a Sixteenth-century Miller*. Translated by John Tedeschi and Anne Tedeschi. Johns Hopkins University Press: 1992.
9 See his 'Global Inequality and Human Rights: a Cosmopolitan Perspective', in *Future Modernities, Challenges for Cosmopolitan Thought and Practice*. Edited by Michaela Heinleina. Transcript Verlag Bielefeld: 2012, pp. 118–19.
10 Ibid.
11 Stephen Greenblatt, *The Swerve: How the World Became Modern*. Norton & Company: 2012.
12 Jean Leclercq, *The Love of Learning and the Desire for God: A Study of Monastic Culture*. Fordham University Press: 1982.
13 Albert Camus, *Essays Lyrical and Critical*. H. Hamilton: 1967, p. 132.
14 Zygmunt Bauman, *This is Not a Diary*. Polity: 2012, p. 2.
15 Ibid., p. 45.
16 Ibid., p. 46.
17 Ibid., p. 94.
18 Ibid., p. 144.
19 ZB's translation.
20 Bolesław Prus, 'Nasze obecne położenie' ('Our Current Situation'), *Kroniki* ('Chronicles'), 20, Tyg.Il.1908, p. 165. SO's translations.
21 Paul Radin, *Primitive Religion: Its Nature and Origin*. Viking: 1937, p. 323.
22 See Mikhail Bakhtin, *Rabelais and His World*. MIT Press: 1968.

23 Zygmunt Bauman, *New Frontiers and Universal Values*. Centre de Cultura Contemporània de Barcelona, 2006, p. 28.
24 Ibid., p. 29.
25 Daniel Boyarin, *The Jewish Gospels: the Story of Jesus Christ*. The New Press: 2012, p. 1.
26 Ibid., pp. 102–3.
27 Daniel Boyarin, *Border Lines: the Partition of Judeo-Christianity*. University of Pennsylvania Press: 2006.
28 Ibid., p. xiv.
29 Ibid., p. xii

VII   God or Gods? The Gentle Face of Polytheism

1 Joseph Ratzinger, *Truth and Tolerance: Christian Relief and World Religions*. Ignatius Press: 2004.
2 Peter Phan, *Being Religious Interreligiously: Asian Perspectives on Interfaith Dialogue*. Orbis Books: 2004.
3 Hannah Arendt, *Men in Dark Times*. Mariner Books: 1970, p. ix.
4 Ibid., p. ix.
5 Ibid., p. 19.
6 Ibid., p. 26.
7 Ibid., p. 10.
8 Ibid., p. 27.
9 Zygmunt Bauman, 'W co wierzą niewierzący (a są tacy?)' (What Do Non-believers Believe In (and Are There Any?)), in *Co nas łączy? Dialog z niewierzącymi niewierzącymi* ('What Connects Us? A Conversation with Non-believers'). WAM: 2002, p. 107.
10 Ibid.
11 Leszek Kołakowski, 'Wiara dobra, niewiara dobra' ('Belief is Good, Non-belief is Good'), in *Co nas łączy?*, p. 13.
12 Stanisław Obirek, 'Dwa oblicza proroctwa. Jan Paweł II i Zygmunt Bauman wobec Europy' ('Two Faces of Prophecy: Jan Paweł II and Zygmunt Bauman on Europe'), in *Dokąd zmierza Europa, przywództwo, idee, wartości* ('Where is Europe Headed? Leadership, Ideas, Values'). Edited by Halina Taborska and Jan S. Wojciechowski. Pułtusk: 2007, p. 132.

Index